BETTER LAWNS
Step by Step

CREATIVE HOMEOWNER PRESS®

BETTER LAWNS
Step by Step

By Joe Provey & Kris Robinson

CREATIVE HOMEOWNER PRESS®, Upper Saddle River, New Jersey

Editorial Director: Timothy O. Bakke
Art Director: W. David Houser
Production Manager: Ann Bernstein

Senior Editor: Neil Soderstrom
Associate Editor: Robin White Goode
Editorial Assistants: Albert Huang, Craig Clark, Laura DeFerrari
Consultants: Anne Halpin, consulting editor and author of
        Horticulture Gardener's Desk Reference
        Tom Schmidt, "The Moleman of Cincinnati"
        Warren Schultz, author of *The Chemical-*
        Free Lawn and *A Man's Turf: The Perfect Lawn*

Graphic Designer: Melisa DelSordo
Illustrators: Vincent Alessi (computer-generated site plans)
        Todd Ferris (tool and equipment paintings)
        Wendy Smith Griswold (structural concept paintings)

Cover Design: Melisa DelSordo
Cover Photography: Lefever/Grushow from Grant Heilman

Manufactured in the United States of America

Current Printing (last digit)
10 9 8 7 6 5 4 3 2

Better Lawns, Step by Step
Library of Congress Catalog Card Number: 98-84957
ISBN: 1-58011-051-7

CREATIVE HOMEOWNER®
A Division of Federal Marketing Corp.
24 Park Way, Upper Saddle River, NJ 07458
Web site: **www.creativehomeowner.com**

Safety First

Though all concepts and methods in this book have been reviewed for safety, it is not possible to overstate the importance of using the safest working methods possible. What follows are reminders—do's and don'ts for yard work and landscaping. They are not substitutes for your own common sense.

❏ *Always* use caution, care, and good judgment when following the procedures described in this book.

❏ *Always* determine locations of underground utility lines before you dig, and then avoid them by a safe distance. Buried lines may be for gas, electricity, communications, or water. Start research by contacting your local building officials. Also contact local utility companies; they will often send a representative free of charge to help you map their lines. In addition, there are private utility locator firms that may be listed in your Yellow Pages. *Note*: Previous owners may have installed underground drainage, sprinkler, and lighting lines without mapping them.

❏ *Always* read and heed tool manufacturer instructions, especially the warnings.

❏ *Always* ensure that the electrical setup is safe; be sure that no circuit is overloaded and that all power tools and electrical outlets are properly grounded and protected by a ground-fault circuit interrupter (GFCI). Do not use power tools in wet locations.

❏ *Always* wear eye protection when using chemicals, sawing wood, pruning trees and shrubs, using power tools, and striking metal onto metal or concrete.

❏ *Always* consider nontoxic and least toxic methods of addressing unwanted plants, plant pests, and plant diseases before resorting to toxic methods. When selecting among toxic substances, consider short-lived toxins, those that break down quickly into harmless substances. Follow package application and safety instructions carefully.

❏ *Always* read labels on chemicals, solvents, and other products; provide ventilation; heed warnings.

❏ *Always* wear heavy rubber gloves rated for chemicals, not mere household rubber gloves, when handling toxins.

❏ *Always* wear appropriate gloves in situations in which your hands could be injured by rough surfaces, sharp edges, thorns, or poisonous plants.

❏ *Always* wear a disposable face mask or a special filtering respirator when creating sawdust or working with toxic gardening substances.

❏ *Always* keep your hands and other body parts away from the business ends of blades, cutters, and bits.

❏ *Always* obtain approval from local building officials before undertaking construction of permanent structures.

❏ *Never* employ herbicides, pesticides, or other toxic chemicals unless you have determined with certainty that they were developed for the specific problem you hope to remedy.

❏ *Never* allow bystanders, especially children, to approach work areas where they might be injured by workers or work site hazards.

❏ *Never* work with power tools when you are tired or under the influence of alcohol or drugs.

❏ *Never* carry sharp or pointed tools, such as knives or saws, in your pockets.

Contents

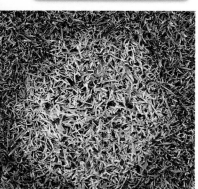

A New Look at Lawns

THE LAWN HAS BEEN THE MOST popular landscaping tradition in North America for over a century. Yet, to a first-time visitor from one of the many "lawnless" nations of the world, it would be hard to understand why people fuss so much over their lawns. The lawn produces no useful crop. It can be expensive and time-consuming to maintain. The chemicals and power equipment used on many lawns waste resources and pollute the air, land, and water. Lawns have the power to inspire otherwise normal adults arriving home after a long day at work to pluck weeds before kissing their kids. And woe to the reputation of the neighbor who neglects the lawn for long.

Nevertheless, lawns have compelling charms. One would be hard pressed to suggest another surface that is as beautiful and functional. Velvety green lawns open views to your house and garden. They take on a glow from a rising or setting sun that can make you feel that all is right with the world. And there's no better surface upon which to kick a ball or have a picnic. The lawn is multipurpose: It can be a badminton court one day and a water park the next.

Is it possible to have a beautiful lawn without devoting more hours and dollars than you can spare? And if so, can you avoid contributing to pollution problems? To both questions, the answer is *yes*. This book will show you how to get started. You'll learn how to redesign your yard to trim away unneeded parts of lawn. Then you'll find step-by-step instructions for restoring an existing lawn; or for creating a new one with grass varieties suited to your climate that grow more slowly and need less watering. Some of the newer turf grasses are resistant to disease and pests, further reducing maintenance needs. You'll also be introduced to irrigation techniques that save water, mowing methods that save time, and slow-release fertilizers that need to be applied less frequently. After the first year of following our program, you will see the time and money you spend on lawn maintenance decreasing. You'll no longer be tempted to pay several hundred dollars a year to a lawn service, and you will be the proud owner of a healthy green lawn without needing to feel any guilt about harming the environment.

A perfect foreground to the striking pelargoniums, boxwoods, and dramatic weeping willow, this lawn shows off their beauty and its own.

Lawn-Care Options

Most people love lawns but find lawn care hard to fit into their busy lifestyles. There are essentially four choices for lawn care: (1) using traditional high-maintenance methods, (2) hiring professional help, (3) doing nothing, and (4) going low-maintenance and environmentally friendly.

High-maintenance lawn care involves five or six applications of fertilizers, herbicides, and pesticides per year, and frequent watering and mowing. Most homeowners can't handle all this on their own, so professional lawn services get their business. But many homeowners question the value of such services. They don't want to lose control over the chemicals applied to their lawns or risk related pollution. Nor do they like needing to keep children and pets off the lawn after treatment.

Lacking time for traditional lawn care, yet objecting to expensive and sometimes toxic services, many homeowners do nothing. They don't apply herbicides or pesticides; they don't use fertilizers, spread seed, irrigate, or worry much about pH (soil acidity). Their idea of a professional lawn service is a local teen doing the mowing.

Fortunately, it is possible to have a beautiful lawn without using time-consuming, costly, chemical- and water-intensive methods. A growing number of homeowners are choosing low-maintenance, non-polluting approaches to lawn care.

Left Woody plants, such as these rhododendrons, low hedges, and dogwood and other deciduous trees, not only frame the lawn handsomely but also reduce mowing. **Inset** Flower borders add beauty and reduce mowing but tend to be more labor intensive.

chapter 1

Lawns Past and Future

HISTORIANS TRACE THE ORIGINS of the modern lawn to eighteenth-century England and France, where lawns became symbols of pride, power, and wealth. England is probably where George Washington caught the lawn bug. America's first president had a huge lawn at Mount Vernon. Thomas Jefferson, minister to the French Court from 1784 to 1789 and a tourist in England during this period, also brought back to the States many ideas about plants and landscaping, including the idea of building his classical estate, Monticello, on a vast lawn.

But the lawn needed well over a century to catch on with the common folk. One reason for the slow start was that America's lawns were even more expensive and labor-intensive than they are today. Having a lawn was feasible only for those who could hire help. Besides, knowledge of grass-growing techniques was limited.

Before 1850, houses were set close to the street and close to each other. Prior to the popularization of the lawn, front yards were more often flower gardens enclosed by a fence and a gate. Farmhouses had what were called front door-yards—fenced-in areas filled with flowers and flowering bushes. Otherwise, the houses were surrounded by pastures and hard-packed earth. In the Southeast, yards were simply earth that was regularly swept to keep insects and snakes away, or they were covered with pine needles.

Major Influences

Many factors combined to persuade North America to adopt the grassy lawn as the central feature of its landscape. For one, the lawn appealed to wealthy landowners who looked to England for decisions about taste. Then too, the estates of Washington and Jefferson set a standard. Even more critical was a mid-nineteenth-century desire to improve the look of both public and private property that, according to reports from travelers of the day, was generally unkempt.

The public park movement and park designers provided early models for landscaping that followed. Preeminent landscape designer Frederick Law Olmsted laid out projects as far-flung as Central Park in New York City and the park-filled city of Minneapolis. His parks favored turf-covered rolling hills, winding paths, and occasional stands of trees.

The Industrial Revolution, with its smokestacks and crowded cities, created a longing for the pastoral ideal. In some ways, lawns and gardens came to symbolize that ideal, making the home landscape a refuge from industrial development.

Other forces that helped to popularize the lawn included the inventions of the mechanical mower (1830) and the sprinkler (1871). Sales brochures of early architects and developers showed homes with lawns. Then too, garden clubs sponsored beautification contests. Lawns became features for municipal buildings, highways, and airports. And lawns were

Above Lawns of early times were maintained with scythes. *Left* George Washington's Mount Vernon estate, along with Thomas Jefferson's classical Monticello *(inset)* helped to create the standard for the suburban grassy lawn.

By the 1870s, the Excelsior lawn mower rivaled the scythe. Youths then, as now, likely preferred other sports.

needed for increasingly popular games, such as croquet, tennis, badminton, baseball, and golf.

It was the pastoral setting for golf, with its wide expanses of turf, that further established grass as the ideal landscaping medium. A partnership that began in 1916 between the United States Department of Agriculture (USDA) and the United States Golf Association (USGA) helped to popularize lawns. The USGA was looking for ways to grow grass for golf courses in regions where the climate was not conducive to existing grasses. In the following decades, the USDA obliged and worked to help develop new grass types.

The gospel of the lawn was eventually spread by the rapid growth of suburbs in the late nineteenth and twentieth centuries. Early suburbs were built for people wealthy enough to leave behind the grime, crime, and chaos of immigrant-filled cities. The ideal of the country estate, surrounded by lawn and trees, was quickly adopted as the standard of home landscaping by the middle class that soon followed the wealthy to suburbia.

After World War II, suburb expansion accelerated across the woodlands and pastures of much of North America. By the 1950s and 1960s, a great mosaic of lawn was growing at an astounding rate. But while lawns were providing a whole generation of teenagers with odd jobs, they were also contributing to environmental problems. With the advent of bagging attachments in 1956, homeowners began bagging their clippings and hauling them to landfills. The number of landfills increased at alarming rates. Nitrates from lawn clippings and fertilizers were running into waterways, where they promoted algal growth and made ponds and lakes look like pea soup. Worst of all was the indiscriminate use of lawn-inspired pesticides—toxins that often stayed in the environment and got into water sources and food chains.

By the 1970s and 1980s, the need to reduce pollution and conserve and recycle resources became clear. But despite the attention focused on environmental issues, lawn-care habits were slow to change. Grass clippings, leaves, and yard prunings still constituted over 30 percent of the volume hauled to landfills. Mowers were still equipped with gasoline engines less efficient than automobile engines. And toxic chemicals were still leaching into water supplies.

To complicate matters, many homeowners during this era turned to lawn-care services to maintain their lawns. In the growing number of dual-income households, there simply wasn't time to devote several hours each weekend to lawn care.

Despite promises from lawn care companies that use heavy doses of pesticides, you're as likely to have lawn problems with their help as without it.

The lawn-care services—which make their profits by doing more to lawns, not less—were happy to adopt the high-maintenance lawn practices of the past on a mass scale.

New Lawns of Today and Tomorrow

Today, there are better ways to have beautiful lawns without wasting resources, polluting the environment, and spending a lot of money on services. New products, from "green" mowers and smart sprinklers to vastly improved grasses and fertilizers, are radically changing the ways we grow and maintain our lawns.

What does the lawn of the future look like? First, it's smaller. Lawn sizes have been steadily decreasing for decades and are likely to continue shrinking. As land has become more expensive, building lots have shrunk. At the same time, the "footprints" (areas covered by houses, garages, decks, and patios) of today's homes are often bigger. Non-lawn landscape elements, such as beds and borders of trees, shrubs, and perennials, are becoming more popular, further reducing the areas set aside for lawns. Similarly, lawn alternatives such as meadow lawns and the use of ground covers in low-traffic areas are giving traditional lawns competition.

Besides being smaller, the new lawn is likely to have more personality than in the past. A new generation of landscaping magazines and books is fueling the idea that lawns, like gardens, can be expressive design elements in the home landscape. They show that lawns can come in assorted layouts and sizes. Some of today's new lawns are formal and geometric. Others are more natural in their design, conforming less to squared-off property lines and more to yard functions and terrain. Today's redesigned lawn may be a focal point in the home landscape, a verdant destination at the end of a winding path. Or perhaps it is the path itself, a green stream that winds between gardens and shrub borders.

With so many people pursuing a greater variety of outdoor activities than in the past, more is being asked of today's lawns. No longer is it just a simple game of catch. Soccer, lacrosse, volleyball, touch football, and Frisbee are demanding rugged turf. Similarly, backyard entertaining is on the upswing. Why fight traffic and crowds when you can have everything in your own backyard "resort"? Pools and spas, even outdoor kitchens, are being installed in record numbers. And it all means more challenges and opportunities for people with lawns.

Meadow lawns devote large areas of yard to flowers and tall grasses. The result? Reduced mowing and a natural, contemporary feel.

This small lawn, bordered with low-maintenance ground covers and cooling trees, helps to create a tranquil spot.

chapter 2

Assessing Your Lawn's Design

FUNNY THING ABOUT HUMAN NATURE. You can become accustomed to nearly anything: door latches that don't catch, windows that don't open, stairs that squeak. That's true in the case of a lawn as well. You can pass by it every day and even mow it twice a week for years without really thinking about it, because you've grown accustomed to it as it is. Does it look as good as it could? Is there too much of it? Does it cost more than it needs to? Is it designed to conserve resources or to consume them excessively and pollute?

The Lawn Design Score Sheet on page 16 will help you assess the strengths and flaws of your lawn's design. It will help you think about how your lawn—and landscape—should look and function. Then you'll be able to turn a critical eye on your lawn and redesign it with pencil and paper. If your lawn design passes the test or if you're happy with the way your lawn is laid out now, you may skip the rest of this chapter and go on to Chapter 3, "Assessing Your Lawn's Condition," page 28.

Design a Lawn for Your Lifestyle

The first step in redesigning your lawn is to list all the ways you now use your yard. Be sure to include projections of your future needs. Don't be concerned if your list is long. Refer to the "Yard Activities Checklist" on the next page to help you along in the thinking process. Then show your list

Families with young children will need to plan for multiple uses.

to other family members for their input. Once you have a comprehensive list, prioritize the activities in order of importance to your family.

Yard Activities Checklist
- ◯ Welcoming guests
- ◯ Chatting with neighbors
- ◯ Storing firewood, trash, toys, etc.
- ◯ Drying clothes
- ◯ Keeping pets
- ◯ Strolling around the yard
- ◯ Flower and vegetable gardening
- ◯ Enjoying backyard sports
- ◯ Providing water activities for children
- ◯ Sunbathing
- ◯ Bird watching
- ◯ Entertaining family and friends
- ◯ Eating outdoors
- ◯ Playing with playhouses or swing sets
- ◯ Parking off-street
- ◯ Exercising pets
- ◯ Other

Do-It-Yourself Lawn Survey: Taking Measure

For the moment, you can put aside your prioritized lawn activities list. The next step in redesigning your lawn is to come up with a site plan. If your property is half an acre or less, measure the boundaries and

(Text continues on page 18.)

Left Beds of shade-loving perennials can replace struggling grass, while reducing mowing and improving the overall design. **Top inset** Ground-level edging allows you to mow without needing to raise your mower blade or return later with a trimmer. **Inset** Low-maintenance deciduous trees and flowering shrubs add visual interest.

LAWN DESIGN SCORE SHEET

Rate your lawn's design by placing a check next to the paragraph that best describes your lawn's condition. Then add up your total points and match that total to the Score Guide on the next page.

Size of lawn

○ **3 pts.** Your lawn is smaller than the non-lawn areas (patios, pools, gardens, ground covers, woods, etc.) on your property.

○ **2 pts.** Your lawn is significantly larger than non-lawn areas.

○ **1 pt.** You have a big yard and it's all lawn.

Shape of lawn areas

○ **3 pts.** Your lawn areas complement the design of your house and garden beds.

○ **2 pts.** Your lawn areas are laid out in pleasing shapes, but they don't enhance your house or gardens.

○ **1 pt.** Your lawn is a series of big rectangles bordered by rows of garden beds and shrubs that don't relate well to your house.

Ease of maintenance

○ **3 pts.** Your lawn is easy to mow, irrigate, and fertilize; it's also fairly level, and there are few mowing obstacles.

○ **2 pts.** In order to complete mowing, you have to make many tight turns, mow close to tree trunks, bend down under low-hanging branches, or move lawn furniture. You need several hundred feet of hose to irrigate your lawn.

○ **1 pt.** You frequently need to traverse steep slopes to mow your lawn, or you need to walk your mower through beds to get to other parts of the yard; as a result, you find yourself mowing the same strips two or three times. Your irrigation plan amounts to praying regularly for rain.

Edge treatments

○ **3 pts.** A grass-free border around the edges of your lawn keeps grass from spreading into your beds and makes edge trimming with a mower quick and easy.

○ **2 pts.** You've invested in landscape ties or plastic or steel edging, and the lawn's edges are tidy but require more than 30 minutes of hand- or power-trimming every week.

○ **1 pt.** The edges between your garden beds and lawn are ragged or nonexistent and are breeding grounds for weeds.

This easy-to-mow lawn has no sharp turns, steep slopes, or obstacles to avoid.

Proportion, or scale

○ **3 pts.** The lawn is an important element of your landscape design, but it does not dominate the property.

○ **2 pts.** The trees and shrubs are dotted at random around the property, not in groups or with other plants. They look lonely, as though someone told them to wait there and then never returned.

○ **1 pt.** Your house and your garden beds seem lost in a sea of green.

Grass species selection

○ **3 pts.** Your lawn turf is dense, with a consistent deep green color and texture.

○ **2 pts.** There are a few bare or weedy patches where kids play their games or use play equipment.

○ **1 pt.** Your lawn has a two-tone appearance, brown and green, for extended periods.

Traffic and circulation

○ **3 pts.** The entrances to your lawn are wide, and you've installed paths where frequent foot traffic is unavoidable.

○ **2 pts.** Your lawn design forces walkers to tread upon the same areas repeatedly, resulting in some bare spots.

○ **1 pt.** Years of parking vehicles on your lawn and treading the same routes have worn ruts and bare dirt paths.

Views from key vantage points

○ **3 pts.** Your lawn provides many attractive vistas as the seasons change, from inside your house and from many vantages around your property.

○ **2 pts.** Your lawn looks good from most vantage points—the windows you frequently look out of, from outdoor entertainment areas, and from your driveway.

○ **1 pt.** Your lawn looks good only from the front access road.

Labor requirements

○ **3 pts.** You spend one hour or less per week mowing, irrigating, and feeding your lawn.

○ **2 pts.** You spend between one and two hours per week on your lawn.

○ **1 pt.** You spend more than two hours per week, or you have hired a lawn-care service.

Cost requirements

○ **3 pts.** On average, you spend less than $150 on your lawn and lawn equipment per year.

○ **2 pts.** You spend between $150 and $250 per year.

○ **1 pt.** You spend $250 or more per year.

SCORE GUIDE

26–30 Congratulations! You have a well-designed lawn.

20–25 You have a fairly well-designed lawn, but you should consider making minor design improvements.

15–19 You have an old-fashioned lawn of the 1950s and should plan to redesign. You don't need to do the entire redesign at once, but now is the time to get started.

10–14 Your lawn design is a disaster! Use the design tips provided in this chapter, or call in a professional landscape designer to help you create a better design.

Above To begin your site plan, draw the boundaries of your property and lawn areas, and write in the dimensions. Measure with a 100-foot reel-type measuring tape.

draw a sketch of the property to scale on a sheet of paper that measures at least 11x17 inches. When drawing to scale, it's helpful to begin with a grid in which each division equals a given number of feet. If your property is larger than half an acre, measure and sketch only the lawn areas, beginning with a sketch of the front lawn.

If you have a survey of your property or a professionally drawn site plan, you can skip the above. Just copy the site lines to paper you can draw on. If you don't have a site plan or survey, it may be

Below left Fill in the details, including lawn, buildings, walks, driveway, patios, decks, fences, walls, trees, and garden beds, as well as their approximate dimensions. **Below** On tracing paper or on a photocopy of the existing site plan, roughly draw bubbles for planned activity areas, such as a patio, children's play area, and intended lawn areas.

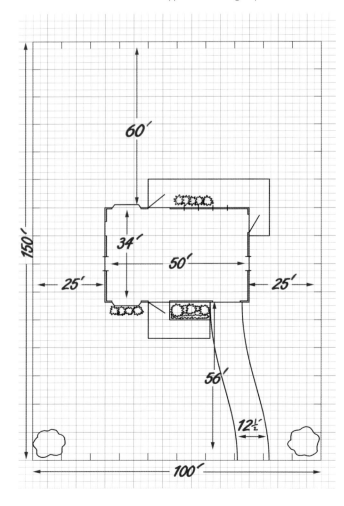

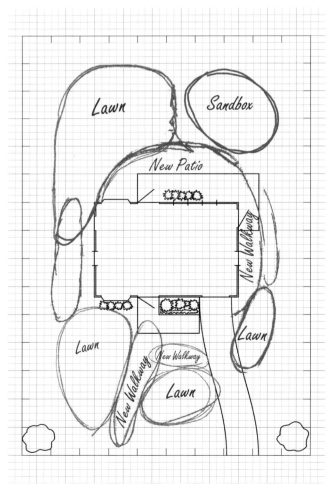

on file at your local building department, where you could make a copy for a nominal fee.

Once you have the outline of the area you're redesigning, begin to fill in the details. Add the lawn areas, footprints of structures, trees and their approximate diameters, garden beds, and other features of your yard, such as pools, paths and sidewalks, driveways, and play spaces.

Then label the areas that correspond to the high-priority activities in the Yard Activities Checklist you completed on page 15. Shade in the approximate area that each activity requires, overlapping those areas that can be used for more than one purpose.

Complete your lawn survey by determining the square footage of each area of lawn on your plan. Add them together to get the total square footage of lawn. Find the square footage of irregularly shaped areas by dividing the shapes into simpler geomet-

ric shapes, such as rectangles, squares, triangles, and circles. Use formulas for finding the area of each shape, as shown in the schematic on the next page. Then add all the areas together to get the total square footage. Don't worry about being exact. You can always estimate odd-shaped areas when necessary.

Replace unneeded lawn with low-maintenance plantings, such as ground covers and mulched trees and shrubs. If you want to save work but still want flower beds, add low-maintenance perennials and annuals recommended by a local nursery. Also, add low-maintenance hardscaping, such as walks, surfaced play areas, and a patio. *Note:* Play areas where children could fall from platforms or swings should be covered with a goodly depth of impact-reducing material, such as wood chips or pea gravel. This material should extend at least 6 feet from elevated platforms and ladders and at least double the height of the swing beam in the direction of swing arcs.

Redrawing the Lines

Now you can begin sketching changes. Lay a piece of tracing paper over your existing lawn plan and start to sketch new lawn layouts. You may need to use and discard several pieces of tracing

paper before you hit upon a layout that begins to look right.

Not sure where to start? Try comparing the amount of lawn you currently maintain with the amount required to support the yard activities you engage in. On your tracing paper, shade in the lawn areas that you do not need. Consider converting these areas to ground cover, meadow, trees, shrubs, or garden beds.

If you have young children, play areas of 5,000 to 7,500 square feet of lawn is probably adequate. Families with older children or no children typically don't need play areas and can make do with far less lawn. If you have significantly more than 7,500 square feet—and do not have special athletic needs, such as hosting the local annual Frisbee tournament—downsizing unneeded lawn areas will therefore save you considerable amounts of time and money over the years.

Alternate uses In your planning, don't go overboard with flower and vegetable gardens if you're interested in saving time and

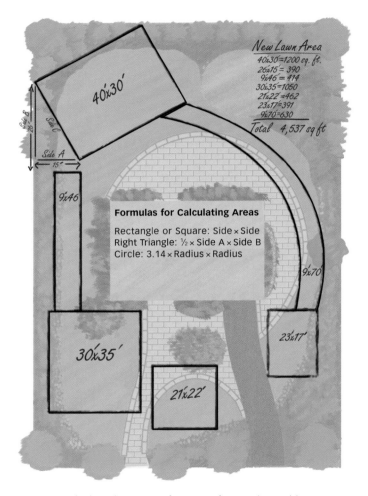

New Lawn Area
40x30=1200 sq. ft.
26x15 = 390
9x46 = 414
30x35=1050
21x22 =462
23x17=391
9x70=630
Total 4,537 sq ft

40'x30'

Side B
26'

Side C

Side A
15'

9x46'

Formulas for Calculating Areas

Rectangle or Square: Side × Side
Right Triangle: ½ × Side A × Side B
Circle: 3.14 × Radius × Radius

9'x70'

30'x35'

23'x17'

21'x22'

To calculate the square footage of your planned lawn areas, follow this procedure: On a tracing-paper overlay, sketch uniform geometric shapes that approximate the actual lawn areas; here, try to create rectangular, triangular, or circular shapes that spacially compensate for overages and shortfalls of irregular lawn shapes.

You can estimate dimensions based on your ruler and drawing scale, or simply count the grid lines on the plan. These dimensions need not be exact, except on areas for which you will be purchasing sod. To calculate the areas of the geometric shapes, use the formulas indicated in the sample drawing above.

This bird's-eye view shows how our theoretical lawn redesign will look. Reduced by more than 60 percent, the lawn is now framed with trees, shrubs, and flower borders that reduce lawn maintenance. Walks avoid traffic-worn bare spots. Property boundaries are well defined with hedges, and the lawn's curved shapes and straight lines complement the house and plantings. The play space invites fun without sacrificing lawn health and beauty.

CREATING NON-GRASS ISLANDS

1 Use a latex spray paint or baking flour to mark the perimeter of the non-grass tree island or bed.

2 Use a spade to cut the turf along the line, and remove the turf with a spade or a grape (grubbing) hoe.

3 After planting the tree, fit the landscape fabric in place.

4 Cover with a 3-inch layer of mulch. But to prevent trunk rot, pull the mulch 6 inches away, as indicated.

money. Gardens generally cost more to create and maintain per square foot than lawns, and they are more labor intensive.

On the other hand, islands planted with trees, shrubs, and ground cover or covered with mulch are less labor intensive than lawn and in time will cost less to maintain.

You don't need to convert large areas of lawn to mulched beds in a weekend—or even in a single year. Begin to convert lawn to alternative plantings area by area, as time allows. An easy way to start is to put in circular "islands" around your trees. This alone can save mowing time and protect your trees from being injured by the mower or string trimmer. For best results with mulched beds, use an underlayment of water-permeable landscape fabric. (See photo inset, left.) Shredded cedar and pine are two good top mulches.

Vegetable beds will reduce the size of your lawn but are far more labor intensive.

Take a long look at the lawn areas remaining on your plan. Remember that a primary function of the lawn is to connect the various areas of your yard, giving it a cohesive look and allowing you free access from one area to another. Look for logical ways to connect the lawn areas to each other and to existing paths and driveways. Connections between lawn areas should be at least 10 feet wide to ease mowing and to prevent funneling of foot traffic to a narrow area. For the same reason, entrances to your lawn from roads, driveways, patios, and decks should also be at least 10 feet wide. Widen or splay the access ways to your lawn if necessary.

More Design Considerations

A good lawn design can help you save money and conserve water. It will also add value to your property and reduce lawn maintenance and pollution. Here are several design goals and solutions to consider for your plan: Prevent water runoff by locating garden beds so that they intercept and absorb runoff from roofs, from driveways, and from elevated lawn areas during heavy rainstorms—or when you let the sprinkler run too long! Doing so will help you avoid sending water and fertilizer runoff into the street and down storm drains, thereby also creating pollution problems.

Eliminate lawn beside streams and around ponds by creating buffer strips of natural vegetation, or plant these strips with species appropriate to your region, and then mulch. The idea is to prevent soil and runoff from getting into open water. Call a Cooperative Extension Service for a list of plants suited to your area. (See page 150.)

Native streamside plants create an attractive buffer zone that both reduces mowing and prevents most lawn runoff from reaching open water.

Assess existing sprinkler systems. Uneven irrigation patterns because of poor design, neglect, or improper maintenance of a sprinkler system may be wasting water and causing stress in areas of your lawn. Systems that overspray walls, walks, driveways, and streets—and onto tree trunks—need to be adjusted. See "Underground Sprinkler Systems" on page 96 for more on lawn irrigation systems.

This low-maintenance planting bed filled with shade-tolerant perennials, including hostas and daylilies, has replaced a scruffy, hard-to-mow lawn.

The curved lines of this naturalistic landscape design create a relaxed look. Installing masonry edging here would make mowing easier.

These path and patio areas provide many access points to the lawn, thereby avoiding compaction and wear in any single spot.

Don't fight nature. Create planting beds wherever grass is hard to grow—whether because of excessive shade, low-growing trees and shrubs, surface roots, or other inhospitable conditions. Your gardens may contain shrubs, trees, perennials, annuals, and ground covers. Shape the beds to relate to their surroundings, and mulch after planting with 3 to 4 inches of a coarse organic material such as shredded bark or 2 inches of a finer material such as bark chips or cocoa bean hulls. *Note:* Four inches is a deep mulch. You'd need this much if the material is light and coarse. But with wood chips, cocoa hulls,

Masonry edging keeps grass out of garden beds, but it doesn't allow close mowing, requiring that you return with a trimmer.

and other finer materials, 2 inches should be deep enough. Three inches is usually recommended if you use shredded bark.
Create low-maintenance edges. A neat edge looks good and helps to bring a sense of order to your land-scape. Ragged, unmaintained borders are breeding grounds for weeds, which can eventu-ally invade the lawn itself.

In addition to a simple edge made with a manual or power edger, edges can be made of stone, brick, masonry, wood, metal, or plastic. The best materials allow you to create

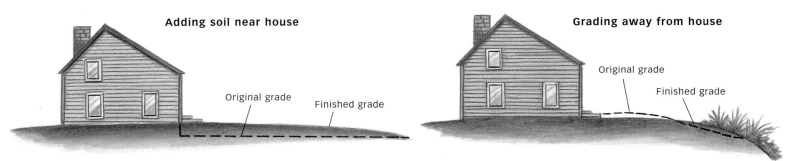

Adding soil near house

Original grade

Finished grade

Grading away from house

Original grade

Finished grade

Ideally, the lawn should gradually slope away from the house, ensuring good drainage, yet remain easy to mow. A slope of 1 foot per 50 feet is generally adequate. This can be achieved either by adding soil near the house (above left) or by grading gradually away from the house and by using graded soil as fill farther out (above right).

Terracing far from house

Original grade

Finished grade

Terracing near and far

Original grade

Finished grade

Terracing is a good way to handle steep slopes. If a lawn slopes too steeply for easy mowing and erosion control, consider trans-ferring soil near the house to the lower level (above left), thereby reducing the slope. The second option (above right) creates a terrace near the house and moves soil from the excavated terrace to the lower level.

TYPES OF EDGING

Edging is a long-lasting boundary that eases close trimming and keeps grass from invading beds. Flat-surface edging of concrete, severe-weather brick, or pressure-treated timbers or 2x6s will let you run the wheels of your mower over it, allowing you to mow the entire edge without needing to return with a trimmer. Sand and gravel underlayments improve drainage and reduce frost heave. Thin barriers of plastic, aluminum, and steel are the easiest to install, and they work well in many situations. But, they may require that you return with a trimmer after mowing to maintain a neat edge. Your principal choices are illustrated below.

Landscape timber

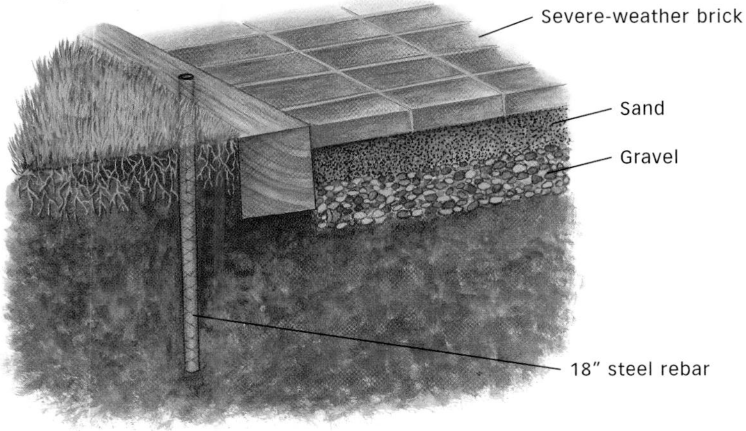

Severe-weather brick

Sand

Gravel

18" steel rebar

Brick on end (8")

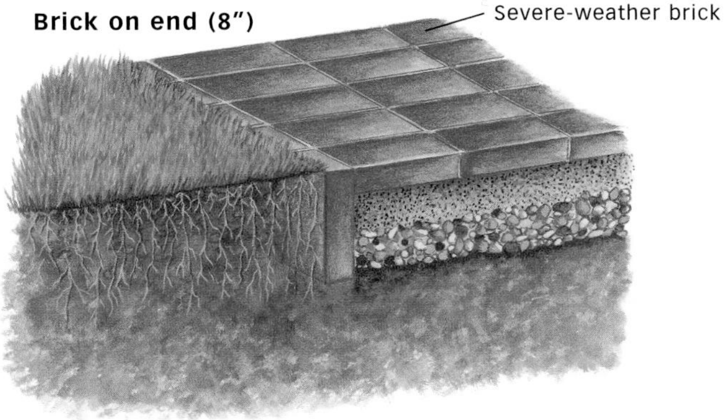

Severe-weather brick

Pressure-treated 2x6

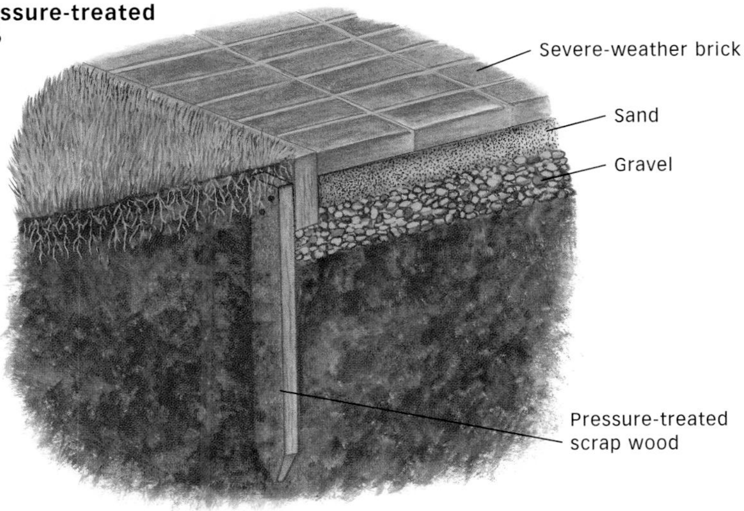

Severe-weather brick

Sand

Gravel

Pressure-treated scrap wood

Severe-weather brick on sand and gravel

Plastic edging

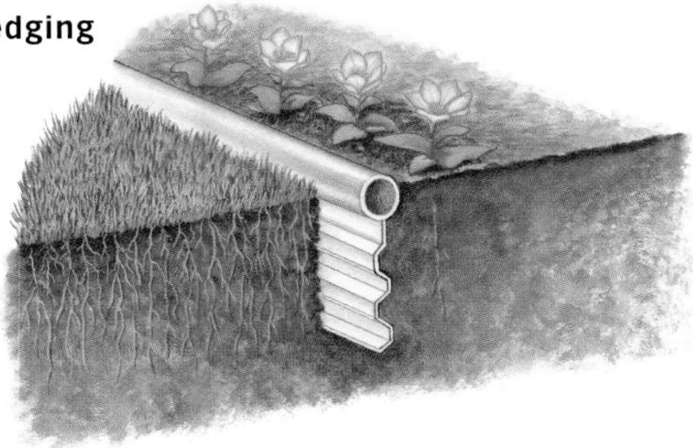

Aluminum edging

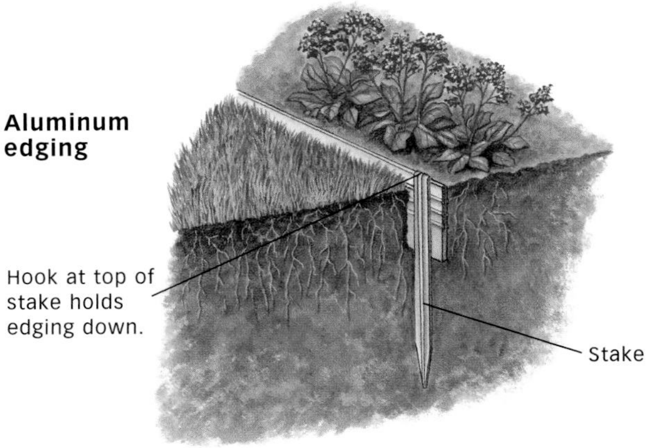

Hook at top of stake holds edging down.

Stake

This terrace created relatively level lawn and garden areas from steep terrain.

Install permanent paths wherever foot traffic is heavy. Stone pavers, such as these shown, need to be low enough so that mower blades don't strike them.

flat-surface edging, which you can mow over without needing to raise the mower blade.

Minimize snow drift. Plant lawn or ground covers beside paths that must be shoveled after snowstorms. Do not plant beds with large woody plants beside such paths or build walls or fences there. Snow will drift to the leeward side of such obstructions, making shoveling more difficult.

Handle steep slopes. Grass tends to do poorly on steep slopes, because it is difficult to establish there and the underlying soil is subject to erosion. Even if you are able to establish good turf, steep slopes can be hazardous to mow. A better solution is to plant a slope with ground covers that require little maintenance and help prevent erosion. Another solution is to terrace the slope as shown on page 24 using materials such as landscape timbers, stone, or masonry.

Install paths. There are two main reasons for installing a path of masonry, stone, or wood in your lawn: to show people where you want them to walk, such as to the entry of your home, and to prevent foot traffic from wearing bare spots in your turf. When planning your lawn, keep in mind that paths require a lot of trimming and weeding along their borders and, depending on the design, between the pavers. Where traffic is low, create a path of turf and define the edges with planting beds and trees.

Create privacy, intrigue, and surprise. The secret of successful landscape design is the creation of a yard that holds a visitor's attention. This is accomplished not only with dramatic plants that have interesting foliage and colorful blooms but also with carefully planned lawn areas. If your yard is big enough, consider creating two or three oases of lawn to create "destinations" on your property. Think of them as hidden outdoor rooms, and plan approaches that obscure the areas until the casual stroller happens upon them.

Show off your garden. Your lawn underlies your landscape design. Use it to separate and give shape to planting beds. Virtually any tree, shrub, or flower looks better against a green lawn.

When designing your lawn plan, think about how it will look from inside your home.

Check out the view. Imagine what your landscape will look like from common outdoor vantage points, such as the street or driveway. Also try to picture how it will look from inside your home.

Know space requirements for yard games. Leave one area large enough to accommodate the recreational activities your family enjoys. For example, an official badminton court measures 20x44 feet and requires a total of 30x54 feet of lawn. A volleyball court is 30x60 feet and requires a total of 50x80 feet of space. Croquet, micro soccer, and touch football can also be accommodated in a 50x80-foot area.

Minimize cleanup. The lawn is a perfect spot to serve cookies and juice to neighborhood kids—there's no need to worry about spills! Grass is also a great shoe scrubber. And a strategically placed lawn helps reduce the amount of dust and dirt entering your home.

Simplify irrigation. Plan and size your lawn areas so that you won't need an elaborate irrigation system. Ideally, use the fewest sprinklers possible to keep your lawn green in hot weather.

This gently winding, welcoming path of lawn separates and shapes the planting beds, which in turn provide color and accent the lawn.

Park on lawn pavers. If you need a place to park your car but don't want to give up lawn area, consider installing lawn pavers. These heavy plastic or masonry blocks of various shapes allow grass to grow between or through them. From most angles the parking space will look like lawn, but you will be able to park on it without damaging your turf.

chapter 3

Assessing Your Lawn's Condition

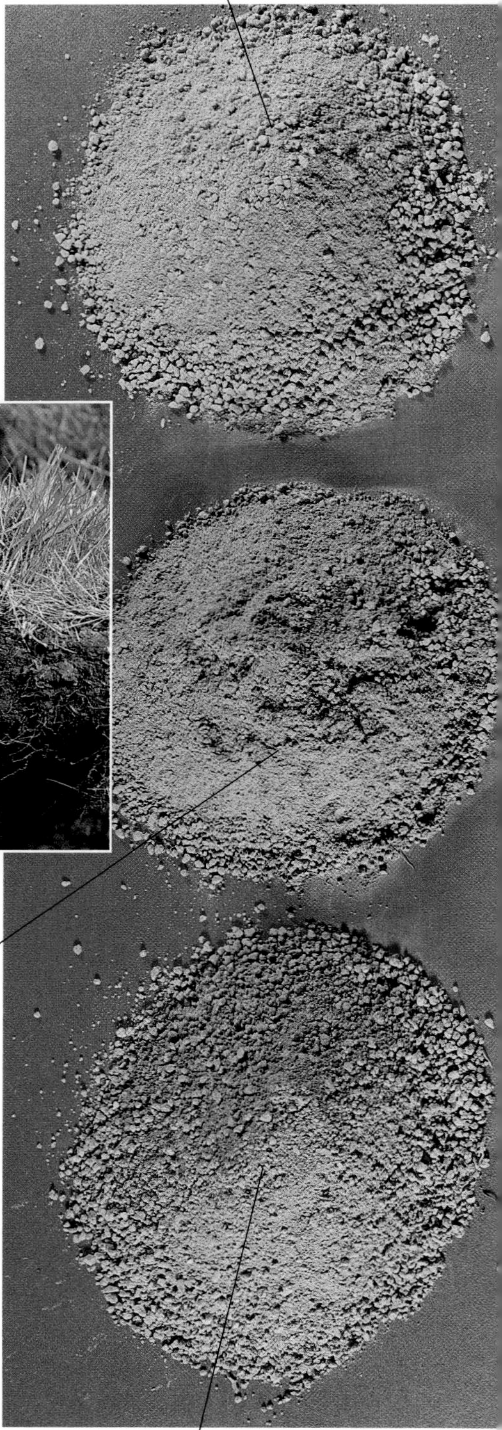

Sandy loam

EVEN THE MOST ATTRACTIVELY designed lawn will not look good if the turf is in poor condition. Take a close look at the quality of the turf in areas that will remain unchanged in your new lawn layout. Is the turf simply in need of nutrients and more consistent maintenance? Is it hopelessly infested with weeds and pockmarked with bare spots? Or, more likely, is it somewhere in between? Depending on how neglected your lawn has been, you will need to decide whether to adopt a new maintenance routine in order to restore existing lawn or to plant a new lawn from scratch. Survey your lawn for the following common problems, and then consider options for solving them.

PROBLEM One
Poor Soil Texture and Structure

Soil is a complex mixture of variously sized particles, water, and air. The particles are mostly mineral fragments generated by the weathering of rocks native to your area. Soil texture, determined by the size of the soil particles, can affect how well suited the soil is to growing grass. Soil particles, from largest to smallest, are sand (0.05 to 2 mm), silt (0.002 to 0.05 mm), and clay (less than 0.002 mm). An ideal

Silt loam

Clay loam

Loamy sand

Loam

Humus

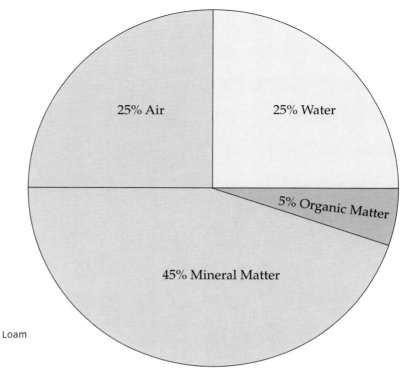

25% Air

25% Water

5% Organic Matter

45% Mineral Matter

Adapted from USDA guidelines, this chart shows the composition of an ideal soil. Applying compost increases a soil's organic matter, which in turn attracts natural aerators such as earthworms and microorganisms. A soil's mineral fragments determine its texture and structure.

soil, called loam, has approximately equal amounts of the three types of particles.

When most of the particles in a soil are sand, the soil can be called sand, sandy loam, or loamy sand and may be too porous to retain moisture or nutrients for long. When most of the particles are clay, the soil is known as clay, clay loam, or loamy clay; these "heavy" soils retain too much moisture, and the soil air that grass needs cannot enter the dense clay. When a clayey soil dries out it hardens, and grass roots have a hard time penetrating it. To find out more about the soil in your region, call your nearest Cooperative Extension Service. (See page 150.)

Soil structure results from soil particles combining to form aggregates. The size, shape, and patterns of these aggregates—ranging from a fine dust to large blocky soil chunks—also help determine relative proportions of particles, water, and air.

Left The size of the sand, silt, and clay particles that make up soil affects how well a soil can sustain grass. **Inset** Granular soil, with a balance of air, water-retention ability, and drainage, helps grass grow deep, strong roots.

TESTING FOR SOIL TYPE: TEXTURE AND STRUCTURE

1 Form the soil into a ball by pressing it between your palms.

2 Bounce the soil ball gently.

3 A ball that crumbles easily may be largely sand; if it stays intact, it may be mostly silt and clay. If it crumbles partially, as shown, it may have a good balance of sand, silt, and clay.

4 Lastly, rub the soil sample between your fingers. A sandy soil will feel gritty; a clay soil will feel smooth and slippery; silt soil will feel smooth and silky.

Between the aggregates are soil pores, or voids, where grass roots grow, water drains, and small air pockets form. Granular soil, the ideal soil structure for lawns, has pea-size aggregates that are neither too fine nor too large, and a balance of air, moisture-holding ability, and adequate drainage.

PROBLEM TWO
Compacted Soil

The greatest enemy of good soil structure in lawns is compaction. Lawn soil often becomes compacted because it takes a pounding: Every square foot gets stepped on as we mow, traipse to the shed or wood-pile, or romp with pets or kids.

Compaction is detrimental for several reasons. First, compacted soil inhibits root development. Second, its original air has been out of the soil, along with the oxygen plant roots need to grow properly. And third, it reduces the soil's ability to retain water.

Compaction also dramatically reduces the population of essential microorganisms in the soil. These bacteria, fungi, algae, and protozoa prepare nutrients in the soil so that the grass plants can use them.

To assess the degree of compaction in your lawn, try pushing a long screwdriver into the turf after a three- or four-day stretch without rain or water. If you find it difficult to push the screwdriver in to its handle, your soil is probably compacted. Other signs of lawn soil compaction include the presence of surface roots from nearby trees, excessive weeds, grass with short roots, and a buildup of dead shoots and roots, called thatch, just above the soil surface.

PROBLEM **Three**
Infertile Soil

Although you should have your soil tested for an accurate reading of its nutrient levels, it's easy to see whether your lawn is getting enough "food" just by taking a close look at it. If the color of your grass is a deep green and the turf is dense, your lawn is in good shape. If the grass is a pale yellowish green and thin, your soil is probably low on nutrients. The presence of crabgrass and plantains may indicate that your soil also has fertility problems.

Test soil compaction by pushing a screwdriver into the ground after a period of several days without rain. The harder you need to push, the more compacted the soil.

Grass plants need more than a dozen nutrients, but most are required in such small amounts that you don't need to worry about them. Three nutrients, however, are required in relatively large quantities to maintain vigorous grass growth: nitrogen (N), phosphorus (P), and potassium (K).

Nitrogen gives grass a deep green color, promotes dense growth, and helps grass bounce back from injury and wear. With insufficient nitrogen, grass yellows and stops growing. Phosphorus fosters vigorous growth and helps young plants establish strong root systems. Grass deficient in phosphorus may be a reddish purple and will have thin, weak leaves. Potassium increases disease resistance and improves hardiness during periods of high temperature and low moisture. Potassium deficiencies may cause yellow veining on grass blades and browning of blade tips.

Because nitrogen is consumed by plants, lost to the atmosphere, and leached from the soil quickly, it should be added periodically. Phosphorus and

The types of weeds in your lawn can give you clues to your soil's condition. Crabgrass and plantains, shown above left and right, may indicate infertility. Buttercups may suggest poor drainage.

potassium bind to soil particles and stay in the soil for years. Except in very sandy soils, they don't need to be replenished frequently. See Chapters 6, 7, and 8 (pages 66–103) for more on fertilization.

Too much of any nutrient can be just as harmful as not enough. For example, excessive nitrogen can reduce root growth and make grass vulnerable to disease. Overfertilization is also a major contributor to water pollution.

PROBLEM Four
Lack of Humus

You don't need to be a soil scientist to figure out if your soil is deficient in decayed organic matter, or humus. Dig up a sample of the topsoil (top layer) under your lawn. Hold it loosely in your hands and note its color. A pale or light color, especially if the topsoil in your area is typically dark, may mean that your soil is lacking in humus—a vital ingredient for a healthy lawn.

Making compost You can build up the humus content of your soil by adding compost to it. You can make compost by piling nonmeat kitchen scraps, disease-free plant matter, or manure in layers in a bin or other container. Later, adding compost to lawn soil will increase the aeration and thus water-retention capacity of the soil. It will also support the highly beneficial microbial life in the soil. For lawn grasses, soil should contain at least 2 percent humus. For illustrated guidance on adding compost to an existing lawn, see page 71.

When filling your compost bin, remember to add equal amounts of materials that are dry and brown, with those that are moist and green. Pile the materials loosely into the bin in thin 1- to 3-inch layers, first of brown matter and then green. Next, add a thin layer of soil (which contains microbes), and sprinkle the pile with water. Your pile should be about as moist as a wrung-out sponge. Keep adding equal amounts of brown and green and sprinkling each layer with soil.

Depending on the season, you may have more green materials (summer weeds) or more brown (fall leaves). Store the dry, brown matter in a tarp-covered pile until you get enough green to mix with it. Newspapers are a cheap, year-round source of brown matter to mix in with your extra green.

BUILDING A WIRE COMPOST BIN

Form one 3' x 8' piece of ½" x ½" galvanized wire hardware cloth or mesh into a cylinder by overlapping about 6 inches of the ends and securing them with four heavy-duty wire twist ties. Then simply place the cylinder on the soil. (If nesting or foraging rodents are a concern, place the cylinder on a paved surface or on a square of hardware cloth or a sheet of exterior-grade plywood. Cover the bin with another square of hardware cloth or plywood.)

Add your raw materials for composting.

When you are ready to turn or use your compost, lift off the cylinder or undo the twist ties and open the bin.

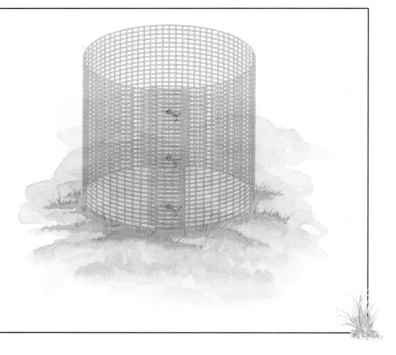

Caring for compost When you have 3 feet or so of mixed green and brown matter in your bin, the material will start to compost, or break down, as a result of the digestive processes of the microbes in the soil layer. You'll know this is happening when the pile starts to heat up inside and eventually shrinks. You can continue to add layers of new materials on top, or you can mix the new materials right into the pile, remembering the half-brown, half-green rule.

Keep the compost pile moist, not dry or soggy. The microorganisms in the pile need both moisture and air to live.

Once your bin is full, you have several choices: If you just let the pile be, you'll have ready-to-use compost in a year or so. If the bin is movable, you can remove it and let the pile slowly decompose where it is. Or, you can have ready-to-use compost in as little as two to six months if you turn and mix the pile. Use a garden fork or pitchfork to mix the pile every week or so until it is reduced in size and is a uniform crumbly dark brown.

No-No's for the Compost Bin

- ❏ Problem weeds that spread by their roots
- ❏ Weeds that have gone to seed
- ❏ Meat, fish, or any food scraps that contain large amounts of fat or oil
- ❏ Large branches
- ❏ Chemically treated wood scraps
- ❏ Dog, cat, or human feces (they may contain disease-causing organisms)
- ❏ Barbecue or coal ashes
- ❏ Glossy paper
- ❏ Things that were never alive: plastic, glass, metal, stone
- ❏ Compost activators—they just aren't necessary

BUILDING A STRAW-BALE COMPOSTER

Attractive and low cost, the straw bales serve first as bin sides and then as recyclable brown material for composting after they age. It's important to use straw and not hay. Straw is the hollow stem of grain after cutting, and these hollow stems allow air to enter, promoting aerobic microbial digestion of the piles. (See photos.) The bales also protect the piles from drying effects of the sun and wind and help maintain the self-generated heat of the piles during colder weather. In mild seasons, you can install a tarp roof to protect the piles from excessive rain. In winter, wood panels can protect the piles from snow and ice buildup. (This straw-bale composter is based on a design by organic gardening author Eliot Coleman.)

Right In summer, the deciduous tree next to the bin shades the piles from drying effects of the sun. In early spring, the leafless tree allows sunlight to warm the piles and reawaken microbial action.

Left Alas, the golden color here weathers quickly to dull gray. *Below* Hollow stems of straw help aerate the compost piles.

BUILDING A WOODEN COMPOST BIN

The single bin being constructed in the photos is easy to make. With this design you have the option of expanding to three bins, as shown in the drawings below, using one bin for fresh kitchen and yard waste, one for decaying material, and one for material that's nearly ready for use.

The three-bin unit requires 12-foot backboards. If you want the optional hinged roof shown in the circle inset below, beef up the rear stakes to pressure-treated 2x4s.

1 These steps show how to build a single-bin composter. For each side panel, cut three pressure-treated 48-inch 2x2 wood stakes. Fasten 1x6 sideboards to the stakes with 1½-inch galvanized screws or hot-dipped galvanized nails, to resist corrosion.

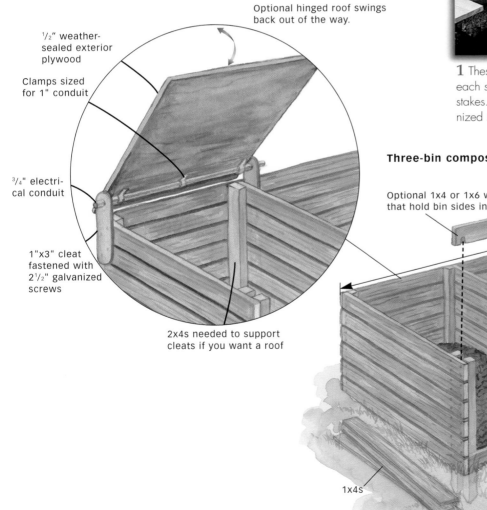

Optional hinged roof swings back out of the way.

¹/₂" weather-sealed exterior plywood

Clamps sized for 1" conduit

³/₄" electrical conduit

1"x3" cleat fastened with 2¹/₂" galvanized screws

2x4s needed to support cleats if you want a roof

Three-bin composter

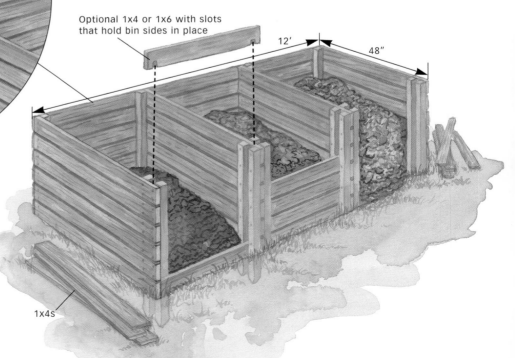

Optional 1x4 or 1x6 with slots that hold bin sides in place

12'

48"

1x4s

2 Cut excess wood from the top of the stakes. Note that the two front stakes are spaced about ¼ inch wider than the widths of the side panels.

3 Drive the stakes into leveled ground, protecting them against splitting with scrap wood. Initially, drive the stakes so the bottom boards are a few inches from the ground.

4 As you drive stakes to final depth, use a carpenter's level to plumb the stakes and level the wall tops. This procedure is easier if you have a helper.

5 Fasten the top backboard with one 1½-inch galvanized screw at each end. Then level the two side panels, as shown, before installing remaining backboards.

6 Slide the front boards between front stakes; do not screw them in place. Add or remove front boards as needed to contain and remove the compost materials.

7 For quicker results, add thin layers of soil, which contains desirable microbes, between the layers of green and brown materials to be composted.

pH AND SOIL NUTRIENTS

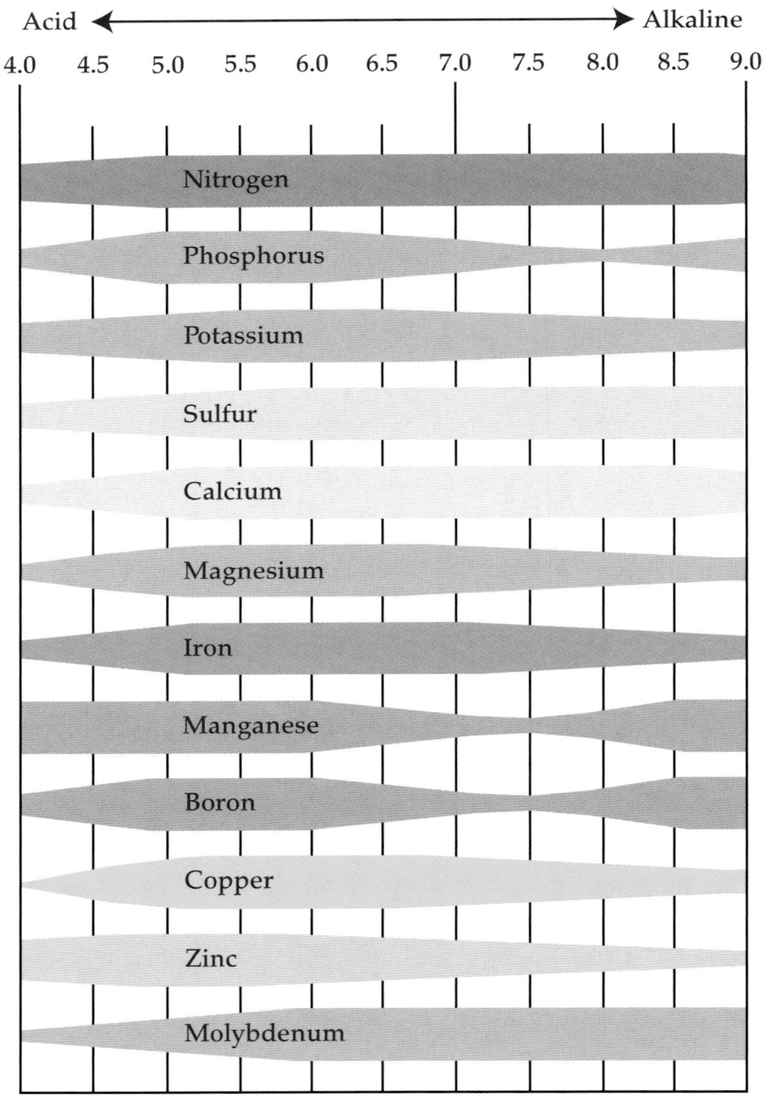

Acid ←——————————————→ Alkaline

4.0 4.5 5.0 5.5 6.0 6.5 7.0 7.5 8.0 8.5 9.0

Nitrogen

Phosphorus

Potassium

Sulfur

Calcium

Magnesium

Iron

Manganese

Boron

Copper

Zinc

Molybdenum

Relative soil acidity greatly affects a plant's ability to absorb nutrients from the soil. For most grasses, the ideal soil pH should be slightly acid, within a range of 5.8 to 6.6. A pH number below 5.5 indicates high soil acidity; a pH number above 8.0, high soil alkalinity.

The bar widths in this chart approximate the availability of essential nutrients at various pH levels. The narrower the bar width, the less available the nutrients. The first six nutrients are needed in larger amounts. Based on USDA charts showing nutrient availability in various kinds of soils, the chart represents only an approximation of nutrient availability in a hypothetical "general" soil.

PROBLEM Five
Soil Too Sweet or Too Sour

Soil that is too sweet (alkaline) or too sour (acid) can spell big problems for your lawn. But short of tasting your soil, which isn't recommended, it's difficult to know which kind you have. Your region and local annual rainfall can give you clues. Most soils in the eastern third of the United States and Canada and along the West Coast are naturally acid. Regions with heavy rainfall tend to have acid soil too. Moss in a lawn is also a sign of overly acid, poorly aerated soil.

Another indicator of acidity is the age of a lawn. Soil that supports a lawn often becomes more acid as the seasons pass. Contributing factors include the decomposition of organic matter, the leaching of calcium because of rainfall or irrigation, and the use of acidifying fertilizers and pesticides. Many central and western states have alkaline soils, resulting mainly from low rainfall.

Soil acidity is measured in terms of pH, or the amount of hydrogen in the soil. The amount of hydrogen, a common element in most acids, is an indicator of a soil's acidity. Soils with a pH below 7 (neutral) are acid, or sour; the lower the pH, the more acidic the soil. Soils with a pH above 7 are alkaline (non-acid, or sweet). Generally, plants grow best in soils that are slightly acid (with a pH between 5 and 7), and grass is no exception. Most grass varieties grow best with a soil pH between 6 and 7 (see chart at left).

A pH change of one point or so may seem insignificant until you understand that the pH scale is logarithmic and not arithmetical. One point on the pH scale indicates a tenfold difference in pH. For example, soil with a pH of 5 is 10 times more acid than soil with a pH of 6.

The pH level of your soil is important to the health of your lawn because it's a factor in determining whether the nutrients in or added to the soil are available to the grass. For example, phosphorus "locks" with calcium and is unavailable to plants if the soil pH is less than 5.5. Similarly, the soil bacteria that break down nitrogen so that plants can use it thrive when pH is above 4.5. Lawns grown in soils with low pH generally have poor color and are less able to recover from the stresses of traffic, heat, and drought.

High pH levels are just as unhealthy for grass as low pH. When soil pH is higher than 8, nutrients such as phosphorus, iron, and zinc become locked with other elements and are unavailable to the grass. When this happens, lawns lose their vigor.

It is possible to adjust soil pH up or down to a moderate extent. Lime can be added to raise the pH of a soil that is too low; sulfur, to lower the pH of a soil that is too high. But before you set about changing your soil's pH, get an accurate soil test. (See Chapter 4, page 42). A soil test is a wise investment, because inappropriate doses of lime or sulfur can literally starve your lawn of nutrients.

PROBLEM Six
Too Much Shade

Excessive shade cast by buildings, large shrubs and trees, or high walls and hedges can make it difficult to grow dense turf. Limited sunlight inhibits photosynthesis, the process by which plants convert sunlight, inorganic compounds, and carbon dioxide into carbohydrates and energy. In other words, too much shade means your grass plants will starve, and starving plants don't look healthy. Shade-afflicted turf has short roots and thin leaves and stems, and sparse, thin growth. This weakened grass cannot tolerate heat, cold, drought, or disease, and it does not compete well with weeds.

As you examine your lawn, note how much sun it gets. Take the time to keep a log, monthly through the growing season, of how long the sun shines on various parts of your lawn. If the lawn receives less than four or five hours of sun a day, your grass is likely to be sparse and may have patches of moss. As mentioned in Chapter 2, you may want to consider converting heavily shaded areas to planting beds. At the very least, you can thin

Sun/Shade Log

Lawn Part: _____

Hour	Full Sun	Partial Sun	Full Shade
6:00 a.m.			
6:30 a.m.			
7:00 a.m.			
7:30 a.m.			
8:00 a.m.			
8:30 a.m.			
9:00 a.m.			
9:30 a.m.			
10:00 a.m.			
10:30 a.m.			
11:00 a.m.			
11:30 a.m.			
12:00 noon			
12:30 p.m.			
1:00 p.m.			
1:30 p.m.			
2:00 p.m.			
2:30 p.m.			
3:00 p.m.			
3:30 p.m.			
4:00 p.m.			
4:30 p.m.			
5:00 p.m.			
5:30 p.m.			
6:00 p.m.			
6:30 p.m.			
7:00 p.m.			
7:30 p.m.			
8:00 p.m.			

To create a sun/shade log for various parts of your lawn, make photocopies of this chart. Then, monthly during the growing season, check off the hours of direct sun.

low-hanging branches, and overseed with a turf seed that's formulated for shade and that can survive on only a few hours of direct sunlight per day.

Too much sun, on the other hand, can cause as many headaches as too much shade. If you're not diligent about watering a sunny lawn, it will burn to a crisp in hot, dry weather. If too much sun is a problem, consider planting low-growing deciduous ornamental trees or tall deciduous shrubs on your property, especially to the south or southwest side of lawn areas. Select a species that grows no taller than 20 to 40 feet and that has an open growth habit that casts light or dappled—not dense—shade. Ornamental maples (Trident, Japanese, paperbark), eastern redbuds, dogwoods (flowering or kousa), yellowwood, and silverbell are all popular choices. The trees will provide some cooling shade during summer midday but will still allow enough sunlight to reach the lawn at other times.

PROBLEM Seven
Excessive Thatch and Short Roots

Push aside the leaf blades of your lawn grass. If you see a light brown, matted layer of dead and living grass stems, shoots, and roots at the base of the plants, you have thatch. Don't panic. Thatch is a problem only when it is thicker than ½ inch. When it is less than ½ inch, thatch can actually benefit your lawn by absorbing impact from foot traffic and acting like a mulch to insulate your soil from extreme temperatures.

A thick layer of thatch, however, can be harmful. It can prevent water and nutrients from getting to the grass roots, encourage chinch bugs and foster diseases. When you are restoring a lawn, thatch of any thickness makes it difficult for seed, fertilizer, and other amendments to reach the soil.

If you find thatch in your lawn, study the thatch and determine how much of the root system is in the thatch. If most of the root system is in the thatch, the roots will be less able to take up and store water and elements used for food production. In healthy turf, roots will reach at least 6 to 8 inches deep.

Thatch can be caused by conditions that reduce the number of microbes and earthworms that would otherwise decompose the thatch; these conditions include highly acid soil, overfertilization, and the use of pesticides. Bluegrass, Bermudagrass, and zoysia are grass species more likely to form thatch than perennial ryegrass or tall fescues. For information on how to remove thatch and maintain your lawn in a way that will prevent its recurrence, see Step 1 in Chapter 6, page 66.

Thatch

Short roots may result if you have excessive thatch buildup. The deeper the roots, the better the plant will be able to support its top growth.

Thatch of more than ½-inch thickness hinders water and amendments from reaching grass roots. It also helps insects and diseases to breed and spread.

This pile of thatch was raked up from a 10-square-foot area. Some grasses, such as bluegrass, Bermudagrass, and zoysia, form more thatch than others.

PROBLEM Eight
Bare Spots, Erosion, and Standing Water

Are areas in your lawn tough to keep covered with turf? Heavy foot or vehicle traffic is usually the culprit. The constant abrasion makes it hard for grass to establish itself, and the compacted soil weakens the grass. Exposure to excessive water flow can also keep grass from thriving. This usually happens at the base of your rain gutter leaders and along the road near storm drains. Standing water that covers the surface for more than four days can also smother and kill the grass.

Wear resulting from foot traffic can often be avoided by installing a path of durable material, such as slate, gravel, or even wood.

Preventing water erosion is more involved. If the source of the water is a roof via a leader or downspout, a dry well will help drain water away. If the problem is running or standing surface water, you must either improve the grading on your property or provide better drainage in the problem areas. (See "Solve Poor Drainage" on page 47.)

Bare paths are a result of heavy foot traffic, which makes grass growth difficult.

PROBLEM Nine
Diseases, Insects, and Weeds

If your examination turns up one or more members of this dreaded trio, don't panic and reach for chemical treatments. Most lawns exhibit some weed growth or small areas of disease or insect activity. This is normal. When kept in balance on a healthy lawn by competition from beneficial microorganisms, fungi, and insects, pest popula-

Some insect and disease activity and weed growth is normal, but fungi and grubs in the lawn may indicate a need to change your lawn-care practices.

tions remain small enough that they aren't considered serious. When a pest does get out of hand, improving your lawn-care practices may be all that's needed to tip the scales back in favor of your turf.

But staying a step ahead of trouble requires that you check your lawn regularly for signs that the problem is either clearing up or worsening. If you suspect you have a problem that improved maintenance alone cannot handle, see Chapters 7, 8, and 9 (pages 76–111). They will help you determine what ails your lawn as well as ways to improve the situation by using least-toxic methods.

PROBLEM Ten
Irregular Surface

An uneven lawn can be unattractive to look at, uncomfortable to walk on, and even difficult to mow. Depressions, holes, and ruts can be caused by erosion, car traffic, or small industrious rodents, such as moles; or by removed tree stumps, buried roots, or logs that decay and cause voids under the lawn. Repair such irregularities before restoring or replanting your lawn.

RATE THE CONDITION OF YOUR TURF

To get a clear picture of your lawn's health, examine it above- and belowground. Don't rely on your memory for this exercise. Walk through your property with this score sheet, making observations firsthand. Place a check next to the statements that best describe what you find. Then add up the scores and compare them with the Score Guide, on the next page.

Aboveground Examination

Health of grass plants

○ **3 pts.** Most grass plants in your lawn are strong and have full blades with a deep green color.

○ **2 pts.** Some grass blades are thin or have a yellow-green cast.

○ **1 pt.** Most grass blades are thin with yellow or brown spots during the growing season.

Turf density

○ **3 pts.** The grass plants form a tight-knit "carpet" with hardly any soil visible; the grass is thick, even where there's foot traffic.

○ **2 pts.** Turf covers the lawn pretty evenly, yet small areas of soil show; some wear shows in high-traffic areas.

Think of your weed-control strategy as two-pronged: to promote healthy grass as well as to reduce weed growth.

○ **1 pt.** Areas as large as 3 or 4 inches in diameter show frequently between grass clumps; bare spots are prevalent in lawn areas used for paths or recreation.

Drainage

○ **3 pts.** Rain is absorbed by your lawn and rarely runs off into storm sewers, ponds, or streams—even after heavy downpours.

○ **2 pts.** Your lawn has several areas of bare soil resulting from erosion, especially near house downspouts; rainwater sometimes seeps into your basement or runs to the street after moderate rainfall.

○ **1 pt.** In addition to basement or street runoff problems, you have standing water on your lawn after rainstorms.

Weed presence

○ **3 pts.** Less than one-fourth of your lawn is infested with weeds.

○ **2 pts.** Between one-half and one-fourth of your lawn is covered with weeds.

○ **1 pt.** One-half or more of your lawn is infested with weeds.

Evenness of surface

○ **3 pts.** Your lawn surface feels level when walked upon; it has no holes or ruts.

○ **2 pts.** There are occasional bumps and depressions.

○ **1 pt.** There are many holes or ruts.

Belowground Examination

Root length

○ **3 pts.** Grass roots are 6 to 12 inches long.

○ **2 pts.** Grass roots are 3 to 6 inches long.

○ **1 pt.** Grass roots tend to be less than 3 inches long.

Soil texture

○ **3 pts.** You can easily push a screwdriver or spade deeply into the soil.

○ **2 pts.** A screwdriver or spade penetrates soil to a depth of 3 or 4 inches before pushing becomes difficult.

○ **1 pt.** It is difficult to push a screwdriver or spade more than an inch or two into the soil.

Earthworm population

○ **3 pts.** There are two or more earthworms in a spadeful of lawn soil.

○ **2 pts.** There is one earthworm per spadeful.

○ **1 pt.** There are usually no earthworms in a spadeful of soil.

Thatch

○ **3 pts.** A ½-inch layer or less of dead shoots, stems, and roots has formed at the base of your grass plants.

○ **2 pts.** The thatch layer is ½–1½ inches thick.

○ **1 pt.** The thatch layer is more than 1½ inches thick.

Organic material

○ **3 pts.** The dark top layer of your soil is more than 5 inches deep.

○ **2 pts.** The dark top layer is between 3 and 5 inches deep.

○ **1 pt.** The dark top layer of soil is less than 3 inches deep.

Earthworms are a sign of healthy soil. They not only aerate the soil, bringing needed oxygen to grass roots but also produce castings that fertilize and enrich the soil.

SCORE GUIDE

30–26 Your turf is in great shape. Proceed to Chapter 8 (page 90) and review the recommended low-maintenance program.

25–20 Better maintenance should renew your lawn. If new lawn-care practices don't improve your lawn's condition, proceed with a lawn restoration, as described in Chapter 6 (page 66).

19–15 Your lawn is a good candidate for restoration, beginning this fall.

14–10 Your turf should probably be removed so that you can improve the soil and replant.

chapter 4

Improving the Basics

Whether you decide to restore your existing lawn or replant it because it's beyond restoration, your first step is to improve growing conditions. Now is the time to make landscape improvements such as grading for better drainage, installing sprinkler systems (if necessary), removing old tree stumps, thinning tree boughs, and felling expendable trees to allow more sunlight. This is also the time to install drain fields, dry wells, paths, and driveways. Once your new or restored lawn is established, you won't want to ruin it by bringing in heavy equipment such as earth movers, stump grinders, or wood chippers to make landscape improvements.

Improve Your Soil

Horticulturists agree that time spent improving what's happening below the surface of a lawn greatly reduces the time needed to maintain what's on top of it. The ideal soil for grass meets five requirements: It (1) is slightly acid, (2) contains an adequate supply of nutrients, (3) allows deep root growth, (4) supports a thriving population of beneficial microbes, and (5) retains moisture. You can achieve these conditions by adding various amendments to your soil. For example, applications of lime or sulfur will modify pH. Fertilizers can supplement the nutrients already in your soil. And organic material can improve soil structure and the soil's ability to retain water and to support microbial activity.

Getting a Soil Test

To learn which amendments and how much of them to add to your lawn, you need to have your soil tested. The best way to test your soil is to send a sample to a Cooperative Extension Service (usually located at or affiliated with a state university) or commercial soil laboratory. (See page 150 for information on contacting your local Cooperative Extension Service.) You can check the Yellow Pages under "Laboratories—Testing" for commercial soil-testing labs. Most test results indicate the pH and nutrient content of the soil, and they will tell you what to add to achieve the correct pH and nutrient levels. Some labs will also tell you what type of soil you have and how much organic material your soil contains. For detailed information on using do-it-yourself soil tests and on understanding soil-test results, see "Do-It-Yourself and Professional Soil Tests" on page 44.

The best time to test soil is in the spring, before you have added any compost or other amendments, although you can test soil at any time of the year.

Kits from soil labs provide instructions for collecting soil samples and a mailing container for returning the soil. Typically, you will be asked to use a clean, rust-free trowel to take samples from up to 10 areas of your lawn.

To collect samples, dig several holes in the lawn 6 to 8 inches deep. Take a slice of soil from one side of each hole, save 1 to 2 inches from the middle of the slice, and discard the sides, top, and bottom. You will then be directed to mix the samples in a clear container, allow them to dry at room temperature, enclose a small fee, and send it all to the lab. Lab tests from state universities usually cost $15 to $20, including the return postage. Commercial lab tests can cost more than $100, depending on the amount of information you request.

Above (three small photos) You can collect soil samples from your lawn areas and test soil pH using a low-cost kit. *Left* Pruning of damaged and unwanted tree limbs can give grass needed sunlight.

DO-IT-YOURSELF AND PROFESSIONAL SOIL TESTS

The costs for multiple lab tests, even at nominal lab fees, will add up quickly. If you need to make more than four or five tests on your property, you will probably want to buy your own soil test kit. Soil test kits range from about $5 for a pH tester capable of doing 10 separate tests to about $10 for a kit that also lets you test basic nutrients (nitrogen, phosphorus, and potash). Kits are available at most garden-supply stores.

These kits are not a substitute for professional soil testing. For example, they do not tell you how much soil amendment to add to achieve desired pH or nutrient levels. The test kits are an inexpensive, quick way to test several areas and will give you a general idea of your soil's deficiencies. Once you have professional soil test results, you may opt to use your own tests to monitor the progress of the soil improvements you make.

1 To test your soil yourself, add the appropriate solution to a measured amount of the soil sample.

2 Shake the soil and solution well.

3 Match the color of the resulting solution with the color chart to determine pH or nutrient levels. The chart here suggests a pH of slightly more than 5, indicating acidic soil and the need for an application of lime.

UNDERSTANDING PROFESSIONAL SOIL-TEST RESULTS

Professional soil tests provide a lot more information than test kits do, but all those numbers and strange abbreviations on lab tests can be confusing. Most include an interpretive key, but the key often doesn't tell you how to implement the recommendations. If, upon receiving a soil analysis, you're unsure how to proceed, phone the source for further help. Below are highlights from one test.

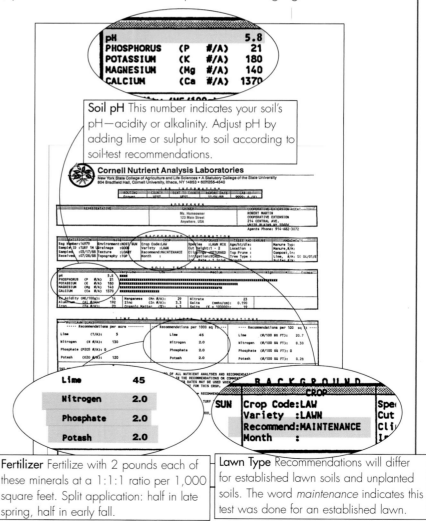

pH			5.8
PHOSPHORUS	(P	#/A)	21
POTASSIUM	(K	#/A)	180
MAGNESIUM	(Mg	#/A)	140
CALCIUM	(Ca	#/A)	1370

Soil pH This number indicates your soil's pH—acidity or alkalinity. Adjust pH by adding lime or sulphur to soil according to soil-test recommendations.

Lime	45
Nitrogen	2.0
Phosphate	2.0
Potash	2.0

Fertilizer Fertilize with 2 pounds each of these minerals at a 1:1:1 ratio per 1,000 square feet. Split application: half in late spring, half in early fall.

Crop Code:LAW
Variety :LAWN
Recommend:MAINTENANCE
Month :

Lawn Type Recommendations will differ for established lawn soils and unplanted soils. The word *maintenance* indicates this test was done for an established lawn.

If your yard has lawn areas that range over various types of terrain (for example, near a pond or brook, a rocky ledge, an area with imported topsoil, or a former garden), you should request a separate sampling kit for each area. Otherwise the lab may recommend doses of fertilizer or soil amendments suitable for one area but not for another.

Test results will tell you what you need to add to your soil. There are two ways to add these materials. If you have an acceptable lawn but are looking to improve it, you may spread these materials over the lawn surface. Chapter 6 covers lawn restoration and explains the best way to accomplish this. It also explains how to aerate the turf with a core cultivator after you've applied amendments. Aeration will help mix the amendments with the top layer of soil and will help loosen the top layer of mildly compacted soils. If your lawn is beyond restoration by mere surface treatment and you have opted to till amendments into the topsoil, turn to Chapter 7. There you'll find step-by-step instructions on how to rebuild soil and replant the lawn.

Let in the Sun

Next, you should prune and thin trees and shrubs that affect the amount of sun your lawn gets. If your grass isn't getting enough sun, it won't look good even if the soil is in great condition and the lawn is well watered and fertilized. While some homeowners are equipped to handle tree-climbing tasks, most are not and should seek a good landscape contractor or professional arborist. Still, light pruning is well within the skill level of most homeowners.

The following guidelines will help you to avoid damaging trees or shrubs when doing light pruning if you take into account their ability to heal their own wounds: (1) When pruning deciduous tree branches larger than 1 inch in diameter, make cuts just beyond the branch "collar" (the raised

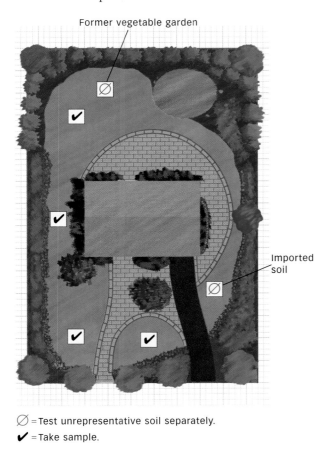

Former vegetable garden

Imported soil

$\varnothing$ = Test unrepresentative soil separately.
✔ = Take sample.

On most residential properties, soil from various locations on your property will be similar in makeup. Unless soils are vastly different, you can combine the lawn samples from various parts of your property for one test. However, if sample sites are likely to have greatly differing makeups—for example, from a highly amended vegetable garden or from an area with topsoil imported from another property—exclude that soil from your lawn test or test it separately.

Thinning upper tree branches is helpful for heavily shaded lawns. A telescoping pruning saw with lopping shears can handle small limbs.

When thinning a tree, carefully select lower branches for removal to avoid ruining the symmetry of the tree. Make your cut just beyond the branch "collar," as shown here.

ridge of bark where the branch joins the trunk). This helps the tree to seal its own wound. Use the three-cut technique on heavy branches to prevent stripping bark from the trunk as the branch falls, as illustrated (below right)—and don't apply paint or other forms of dressing to the wound. Recent research has shown that applying a dressing may actually promote tree decay by sealing in harmful microorganisms. (2) When pruning small branches, always prune back to a bud or to another branch. (3) Make the cut at the angle of the bud or remaining branch, taking care not to injure either one.

The best time to prune most live branches is in late winter or early spring, when most trees and shrubs are dormant, and before new growth starts.

These buds will become branches. Prune at the angle of the farthest bud in which you wish to encourage growth and about ¼ inch beyond it.

Pruning at this time promotes better healing and enables the plant to send out new growth the following spring. Avoid pruning trees producing high amounts of sap, such as maples and birches, after January. Later, if necessary, trees can be pruned in summer or fall, but be sure to keep summer pruning moderate, because that's when sap-producing trees and most plants are producing food. In general, avoid pruning in the spring.

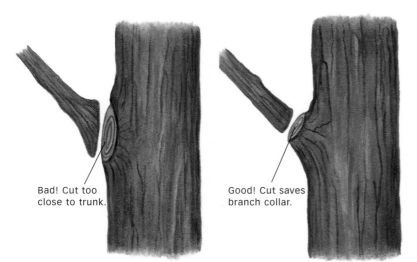

Bad! Cut too close to trunk.

Good! Cut saves branch collar.

When pruning tree branches, many people mistakenly cut too far back into live wood, as shown at left, exposing the wound to insects and disease a long time before bark can grow over it, if ever. Instead, cut back just to the outer portion of the swollen branch collar, as shown at right. The branch collar has cells and chemicals that block decay and diseases in a process known as *compartmentalization*.

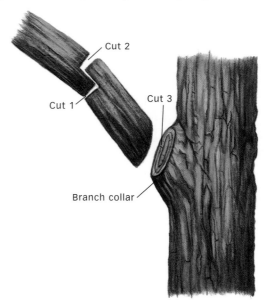

Cut 2

Cut 1

Cut 3

Branch collar

To avoid stripping bark from a tree when the cut limb falls, use this three-step cutting method: (1) Undercut the limb about a foot out from your final cut. (2) Make the second cut from the top, a little farther out on the branch, allowing the limb to break off cleanly. (3) After most of the branch has fallen away, trim off the branch stub just above the outside of the branch collar.

Remove Stumps

Removing small stumps up to 10 inches in diameter using a spade and ax is called grubbing. This requires strength and perseverance. First, dig a 1- to 2-foot-wide trench around the stump, 1 to 2 feet deep. As you encounter roots, expose and cut them, using a pruning saw, lopping shears, or ax. Continue to dig until you can insert a steel bar or shovel under the mass of roots. Pry on all sides, and continue to dig and cut newly exposed roots. On a tree with a significant taproot, you may need to dig deeper. Lean the root mass to one side and cut the taproot as deep as possible. The stump will gradually break loose from the soil. For quick removal of larger stumps, either rent a stump grinder or hire a tree-removal professional.

Solve Poor Drainage

Solving minor drainage problems is something most homeowners can do. The most common drainage problem is water that runs off steep slopes, roofs, and driveways. Water that runs across the surface of your lawn can erode soil and wash away any grass that's trying to establish itself.

Roof water is commonly directed away from the house and basement by a system of fascia gutters and downspouts called leaders. If your lawn shows signs of erosion at the leaders, dig a trench about 2 feet deep, 3 feet wide, and 6 feet long from the leader out into the lawn. Save any reusable sod. Then fill the trench with

1 After removing the turf, dig a trench around the stump; then use an ax and lopping shears to sever roots as you uncover them.

2 Continue to remove soil until you reach the underside of the root mass. A heavy-duty lopper can make quick work of roots up to about 1½ inches in diameter.

3 Dig around and under the stump, using a spade to loosen and test-wiggle the root mass.

4 If there are roots you cannot reach, a whack with a sledgehammer will often break the stump free.

5 Lastly, work a shovel or steel bar under the root mass to free the stump.

48

SOLVING DRAINAGE PROBLEMS

Below are four options for redirecting surface water, roughly in the order of their cost and their capacity for volume, from most to least. A subsurface trench can serve as a major conduit if its cross section is large enough. An open rock swale can handle relatively heavy flows, while preventing erosion. A mowable swale functions best if surface soil is relatively impermeable, thereby keeping water at or near the lawn surface. An earthen berm functions much like a mowable swale.

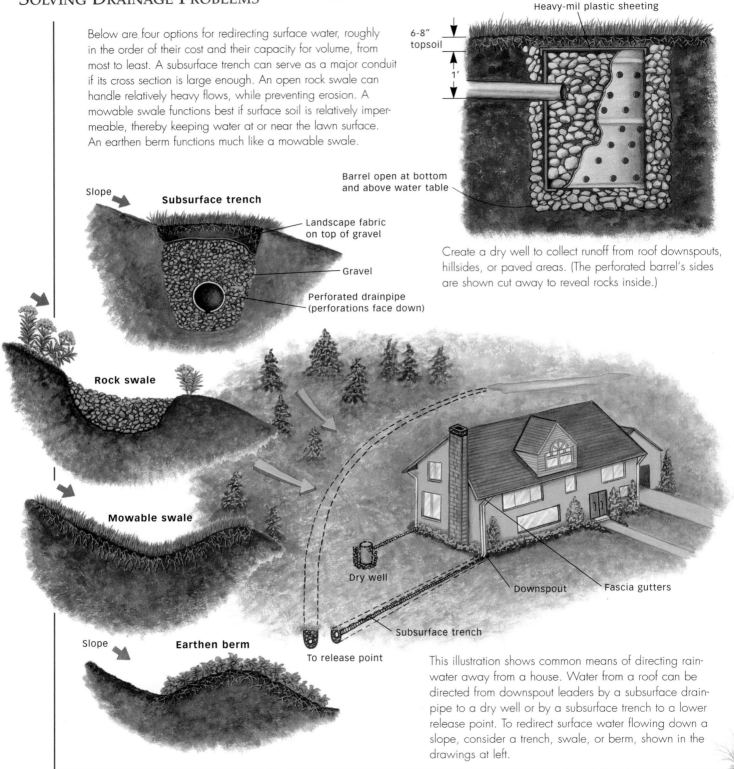

Heavy-mil plastic sheeting

6-8" topsoil

1'

Barrel open at bottom and above water table

Slope

Subsurface trench

Landscape fabric on top of gravel

Gravel

Perforated drainpipe (perforations face down)

Create a dry well to collect runoff from roof downspouts, hillsides, or paved areas. (The perforated barrel's sides are shown cut away to reveal rocks inside.)

Rock swale

Mowable swale

Slope

Earthen berm

Dry well

Downspout

Fascia gutters

Subsurface trench

To release point

This illustration shows common means of directing rainwater away from a house. Water from a roof can be directed from downspout leaders by a subsurface drainpipe to a dry well or by a subsurface trench to a lower release point. To redirect surface water flowing down a slope, consider a trench, swale, or berm, shown in the drawings at left.

¼-inch gravel to a depth of 1½ feet, and cover with water-permeable landscape fabric and topsoil. The landscape fabric will keep the gravel bed from getting plugged with topsoil. Replant the affected area with sod or reseed it. Put a splash block, available at home centers, directly under the leader. Or, install a dry well under the leaders—a better alternative if you are dealing with a large volume of water.

For houses without gutters, experts recommend constructing a drip zone that begins under the roof eaves and extends several feet from the house. This zone is constructed similarly to the trench described for a downspout in the previous paragraph, except that this zone is usually filled with stones or gravel and covered with mulch.

If the grade or slope of your land causes rainfall to flow toward your house or to low-lying areas where you are trying to grow grass or establish a garden, consult a landscape architect or designer with experience in your locale; solving drainage problems resulting from poor grading can be tricky. A pro will begin with percolation tests, which show areas that are slow to drain, indicating where you may need a subsurface drainage system, as shown on the previous page. Lawns with steep slopes to the road (a drop greater than 1 foot over 50 feet) may be subject to bare spots resulting from erosion. They also waste rainwater by directing it to storm sewers before it can be absorbed by the soil. One solution is

This sloped soil being excavated by heavy equipment once wasted heavy rain runoff by carrying it to the street's storm drain.

The soil is used as fill behind the new retaining wall. Plantings will catch the runoff.

to use an oblong planting bed as a water trap. Placed at the foot of the slope, the bed will catch the runoff and, if well-mulched, will rarely need watering.

By now you have a good idea of how to set the stage for your new or improved lawn. The next chapter will help you choose the grass seed mix or blend best suited to your needs. If your lawn was established before 1990, it will benefit from the new grass types vigorous enough to crowd out weeds, tolerate stress, and resist insects and diseases. If you have decided to restore your lawn, proceed to Chapter 7 (page 76). If you have instead decided to plant a new lawn, proceed to Chapter 6 (page 66).

Splash blocks direct downspout water a few feet away from the foundation, helping start the flow downslope.

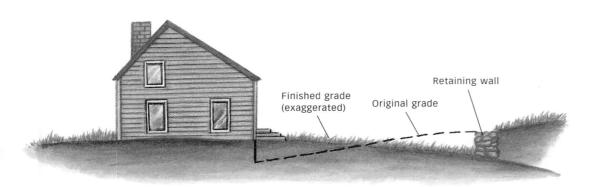

Finished grade (exaggerated)

Original grade

Retaining wall

If the existing lawn slopes toward your house, causing water problems at the house foundation, consider lowering the grade farther out and raising the grade near the house. In this case, a masonry retaining wall can help you provide reasonably level mowing on both sides.

chapter 5

Choosing the Right Grass

Bunch-forming

D ON'T BUY SEED ON IMPULSE! Choosing the right grass for your yard can make the difference between having a low-maintenance, environmentally friendly lawn and one that is susceptible to disease, pests, and weed invasion and that requires a lot of upkeep. The type of seed you choose for either a new or restored lawn should depend on several factors. First, what do you want your lawn to look like? Grasses vary in color, leaf width, habit (characteristic appearance), and density of growth. Second, how much time and money are you realistically willing to spend tending your lawn? Higher-maintenance grasses mean greater cost and time commitments. Third, your seed choice will be affected by your site's growing conditions: the amount of sun and shade your site gets, the soil type and its level of fertility and dryness or wetness, and your climate. Finally, consider how your lawn will be used: for decorative landscaping, for erosion control, or as a play area. After considering these questions, continue reading this chapter to learn more about variations in grass growth and appearance.

Basic Distinctions in Grasses

Different species of grass have distinctive growth habits that will affect the appearance of turf. Bunch grasses, such

Rhizome-forming

Rhizome

Stolon-forming

Stolon

as ryegrasses and most fescues, don't spread but enlarge through the growth of sideshoots, or *tillers*. Bunch grasses are easy to spot if your lawn thins out, because they look like small clumps or islands arising from the same crown. They wear well, but they don't form a solid sod, and you may need to overseed frequently to fill in areas of die-off.

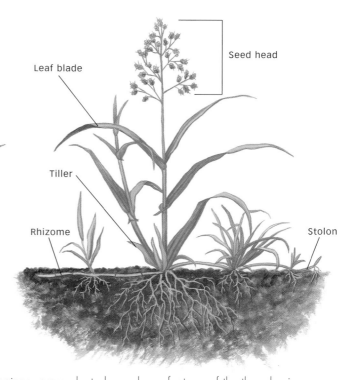

Seed head

Leaf blade

Tiller

Rhizome

Stolon

The imaginary grass plant above shows features of the three basic types of grass before going to seed: bunch grasses, stolon-forming grasses, and rhizome-forming grasses. If not allowed to go to seed, some grasses spread by only one of the three means. Other grasses employ a combination of the three. Although grass experts often prefer to identify grasses based on features in the seed heads, some can identify grasses based only on features from the cut blades downward.

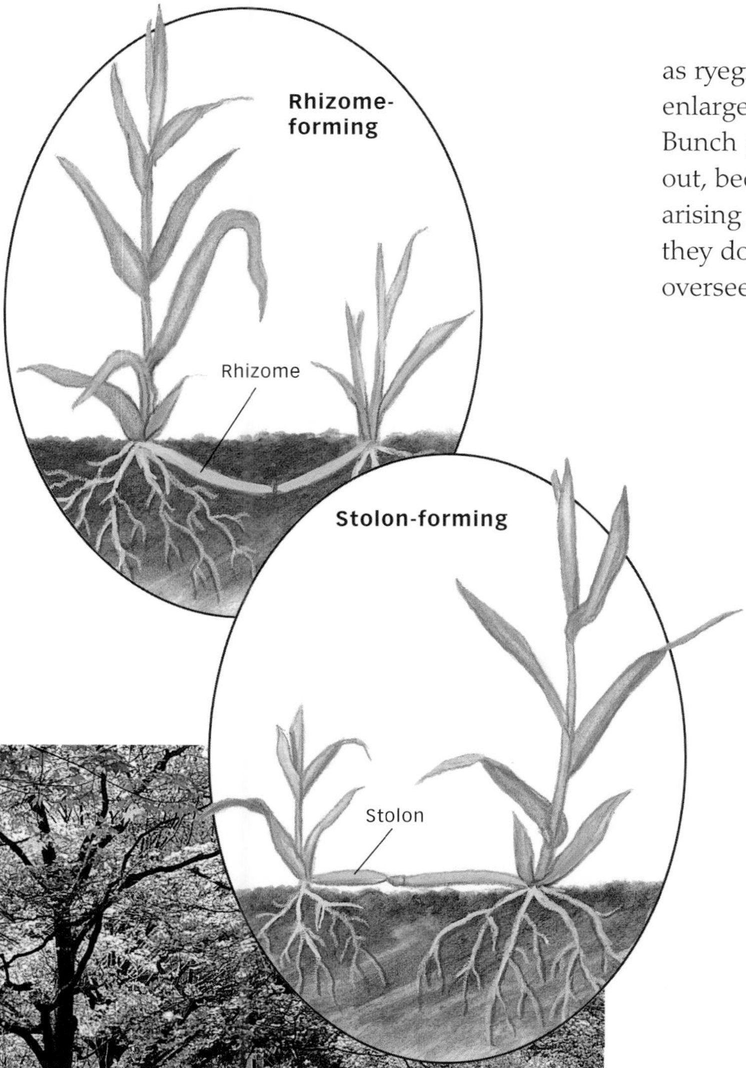

Drawings in ovals Like other plants, grass can reproduce from its own seed. But lawn grasses are typically mowed before producing seed. You may want to select a grass or combination of grasses that spread by one or more of the means illustrated here and on the next page. *Left* If you have a shady yard, choose shade-tolerant grasses for your lawn. But even shade-tolerant grasses need two to four hours of direct sunlight daily.

Kentucky bluegrass and red fescues spread by a combination of underground runners, or rhizomes; and sideshoots, or tillers.

Centipedegrass spreads by aboveground runners called stolons.

Tiller

Bunch grasses, such as ryegrass, tall fescues, and crested wheatgrass, spread by means of tillers.

Some other grasses have *rhizomes*, underground runners that extend out to create new plants. Kentucky bluegrass spreads this way, which is why it's planted in mixtures along with bunch grasses. Having rhizomes, it forms strong sod and is able to quickly regrow into injured areas.

Other types of grass spread by developing new plants from aboveground runners, known as *stolons*. This is typical of the vigorous growth of many southern grasses and explains why they frequently crowd out other grasses and weeds. Certain grasses, such as zoysia and creeping fescue, use a combination of these methods to expand. Lastly, if mature seed heads are not mowed off,

This shows texture differences between tall fescue (wide blades) and perennial ryegrass after summer drought stress.

some grasses are likely to spread through dispersal of their own seed.

Variations in Texture

A key characteristic of grass is its texture. Determined by the width of individual grass blades, texture ranges from coarse to fine. Both fine fescues and bluegrasses have narrow blades described as providing a "carpetlike" lawn. Bentgrass, another fine-leaved species, makes up the velvetlike greens on golf courses. Unless you want a putting green, don't try to replicate this look. The high level of care bentgrass requires makes it unsuitable for most home lawns.

A grass that is termed coarse has wider blades and doesn't necessarily wear better. Tall fescues in the North, and St. Augustine, bahiagrass, and centipede-grass in the South, are considered coarse. Just to keep things interesting, blade texture can vary by cultivar within the same species. Zoysiagrass is a prime example: 'Emerald' is fine-textured, 'Meyer' is medium, and 'Sunrise' is coarse!

A Rainbow of Greens

Color is another important characteristic of grass. There are many variations on the theme of green, from bluish gray to apple green. This wouldn't matter much except that at some point you're apt to be combining different grasses, and for the sake of uniformity, you'll be happier if they blend well. Check for color descriptions on seed labels. When in doubt, ask your Cooperative Extension Service or a local nursery manager.

Other Important Characteristics

Also consider a turf's density and shade tolerance. Density refers to the number of leaves or shoots growing in an area. A healthy and mature cool-season lawn averages six to eight grass plants per square inch. Finer-leaved grasses, like fine fescues, generally produce denser and more uniform lawns

Dense turf crowds out weeds and supports traffic better than sparse turf.

in the North. In the South, Bermudagrass and zoysiagrass exhibit high-density growth.

Shade should be a major consideration in choosing grass. Fine fescue, the most shade-tolerant cool-season grass, still needs two to four hours of direct sunlight a day. Shade-tolerate grasses also require different management than sun-loving species. (See "Cool-Season Grasses" and "Warm-Season Grasses" for shade-tolerant grass types.)

Cool Season versus Warm Season

There is yet to be bred a grass able to thrive on Vermont ski slopes and amid Florida orange trees. For this reason, grasses are divided into two main groups, *cool-season* and *warm-season*, and divided further into two subgroups, *native* and *transitional zone*. The cool-season grasses all thrive in northern areas, including Canada, and in higher elevations farther south. Their main growth period is in spring and fall when soil temperatures are 50° to 65°F, and the air temperature is 60° to 75°F. Come high summer they usually go dormant unless they are kept under regular irrigation. Kentucky bluegrass, bentgrass, ryegrass, and the fescues are all cool-season grasses.

Warm-season grasses grow best in southern regions and rev up their growth along with the increasing heat of summer. Growing strongly when soil temperatures are between 70° and 90°F, and the air is a balmy 80° to 95°F, they become dormant with the onset of cooler weather. The degree of cold tolerance of warm-season grasses varies by cultivar, but many turn straw-colored or light brown after the first frost. The Bermuda, St. Augustine, and zoysia grasses are just a few in this group. Some grasses can adapt to the climate in the band across the country where North meets South, or the transitional zone. Depending on whom you ask, this zone extends from southern California, east through Oklahoma and Kansas, to the eastern coastal states of Virginia, the Carolinas, and Georgia.

Tall fescues and zoysiagrass are the two grasses most frequently used in this transitional area.

Native, or prairie, grasses are those adapted to the arid conditions of the Great Plains. Drought resistance and a preference for neglect are their most desirable qualities. Buffalograss, wheatgrass, and blue grama are all native grasses that do well under these conditions.

Perennial versus Annual Grasses

The penalty for not knowing whether your grass is a perennial or merely an annual may be disap-pointment when your lawn dies out after one growing season. Given appropriate conditions, grass labeled as perennial will persist year after year. Although annual grasses generally last for just one season, they are prized for their fast and vigorous growth. This makes them a good cover crop that prevents erosion.

Annual grasses are also used as nurse, or com-panion, grasses to shade perennial grasses that have slower-growing seed. In the South, annual ryegrasses are sometimes used to overseed warm-season grasses, providing green color during the latter's winter dormancy.

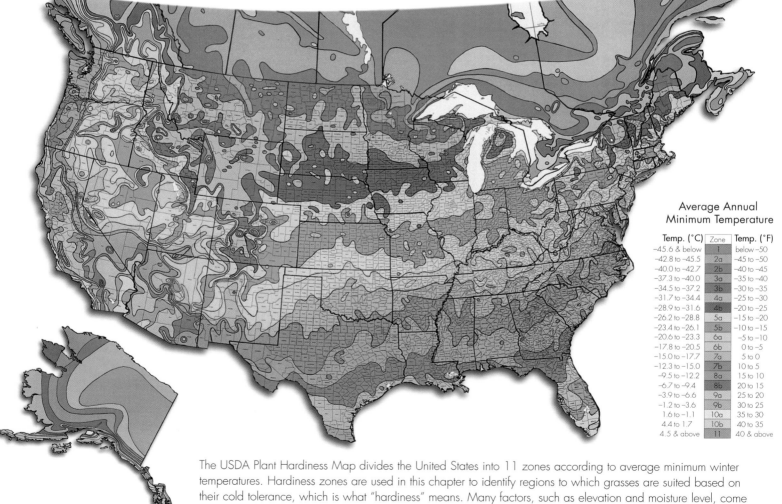

Average Annual Minimum Temperature

Temp. (°C)	Zone	Temp. (°F)
−45.6 & below	1	below −50
−42.8 to −45.5	2a	−45 to −50
−40.0 to −42.7	2b	−40 to −45
−37.3 to −40.0	3a	−35 to −40
−34.5 to −37.2	3b	−30 to −35
−31.7 to −34.4	4a	−25 to −30
−28.9 to −31.6	4b	−20 to −25
−26.2 to −28.8	5a	−15 to −20
−23.4 to −26.1	5b	−10 to −15
−20.6 to −23.3	6a	−5 to −10
−17.8 to −20.5	6b	0 to −5
−15.0 to −17.7	7a	5 to 0
−12.3 to −15.0	7b	10 to 5
−9.5 to −12.2	8a	15 to 10
−6.7 to −9.4	8b	20 to 15
−3.9 to −6.6	9a	25 to 20
−1.2 to −3.6	9b	30 to 25
1.6 to −1.1	10a	35 to 30
4.4 to 1.7	10b	40 to 35
4.5 & above	11	40 & above

The USDA Plant Hardiness Map divides the United States into 11 zones according to average minimum winter temperatures. Hardiness zones are used in this chapter to identify regions to which grasses are suited based on their cold tolerance, which is what "hardiness" means. Many factors, such as elevation and moisture level, come into play when determining whether a grass is suitable for your region. Local climates may vary from what is shown on this map. Contact your local Cooperative Extension Service for seed recommendations for your area.

Which Grass Where?

If you peruse the research reports of various grass institutes, you will be astonished at the number of cultivars of grass species. When you throw into the equation the numerous characteristics of each grass and how each grows under different conditions, the task of selecting the best choice for your location and intended use can seem daunting. Before you despair, phone your Cooperative Extension Service and speak with a turf grass specialist. Other excellent resources for those who enjoy wading through comparison charts are the National Turfgrass Evaluation Program (NTEP) and the Guelph Turfgrass Institute in Ontario, Canada. Using the Internet, you can access much of this information from home. Check "Appendix II" on page 150 for postal and e-mail addresses.

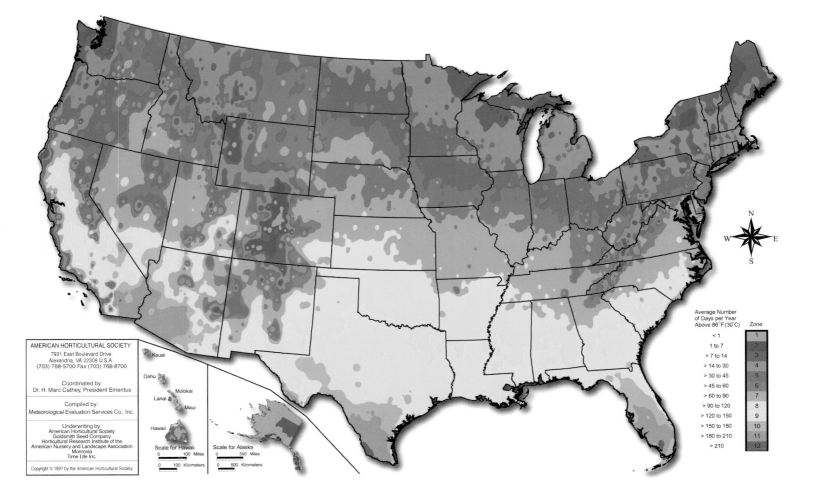

AMERICAN HORTICULTURAL SOCIETY
7931 East Boulevard Drive
Alexandria, VA 22308 U.S.A.
(703) 768-5700 Fax (703) 768-8700

Coordinated by:
Dr. H. Marc Cathey, President Emeritus

Compiled by:
Meteorological Evaluation Services Co., Inc.

Underwriting by:
American Horticultural Society
Goldsmith Seed Company
Horticultural Research Institute of the
American Nursery and Landscape Association
Monrovia
Time Life Inc.

Copyright © 1997 by the American Horticultural Society

Average Number of Days per Year Above 86°F (30°C)	Zone
< 1	1
1 to 7	2
> 7 to 14	3
> 14 to 30	4
> 30 to 45	5
> 45 to 60	6
> 60 to 90	7
> 90 to 120	8
> 120 to 150	9
> 150 to 180	10
> 180 to 210	11
> 210	12

The American Horticultural Society Heat-Zone Map divides the United States into 12 zones based on the average annual number of days a region's temperatures climb above 86°F (30°C), the temperature at which the cellular proteins of plants begin to experience injury. Introduced in 1998, the AHS Heat-Zone Map holds significance, especially for gardeners in southern and transitional zones. Nurseries, growers, and other plant sources will gradually begin listing both cold hardiness and heat tolerance zones for plants, including grass plants. Using the USDA Plant Hardiness map, which can help determine a plant's cold tolerance, and the AHS Heat-Zone Map, gardeners will be able to safely choose grasses that tolerate their region's lowest and highest temperatures.

Purchasing Seed

There are two ways to purchase grass seed. You can visit the garden section of a retail store and pick out a package labeled with intended use, such as "Shade Mix." Or, you can buy the latest cultivars and make up your own mix. For this you will need to nose around, starting with a good nursery. If the nursery doesn't carry what you want, staff there can probably suggest where to shop. Calling the customer service departments of the large seed producers should also yield results. Either way, you will still need to know the basics about purchasing seed, beginning with the terms *species* and *cultivar*.

The word *species* refers to a group of closely related plants that differ from one another in only minor ways. Tall fescues are one species of lawn grass. The various members of a species are called varieties (which originally occurred in nature) or cultivars (*vari*ations that came about in *culti*vation, as a result of deliberate breeding). In common usage the terms *variety* and *cultivar* are often interchanged, but there is a difference between them.

Grass cultivars include old standbys, such as the tall fescues 'Alta' or 'Kentucky 31', as well as new and improved types that have been bred and chosen for superior characteristics. Newer grass cultivars, in most cases, are highly recommended.

Mixtures and Blends

Cool-season grasses are frequently packaged in either a mixture or a blend. Mixtures have two or more species of grass, and blends contain two or more cultivars of the same species. There are many advantages to planting a mixture or blend. For one thing, the turf will be more resistant to diseases and pests, because each cultivar or species has its own strengths and weaknesses. And since most lawns have a variety of growing conditions, the different grasses can grow where they are best adapted within your lawn.

In a typical mixture containing bluegrass, ryegrass, and fine fescue, the fescues will thrive in the shady portion of the lawn, while the bluegrass

WHAT'S IN A NAME?

Many people are familiar with common grass names such as Kentucky bluegrass. In addition, grass plants (like all plants) have two-part botanical names. While the mere use of such scientific names makes most people tune out, the fact is, they can be helpful, even to nonscientists.

First, botanical names pop out because they are usually italicized or underlined. The first italicized word, the genus, is capitalized and indicates a group of species that have similar structural parts. The second italicized word is the species, which is not capitalized, and indicates like plants that can interbreed true to their parents. Knowing that Kentucky bluegrass is also called *Poa pratensis* allows you to identify other plants from the same genus and species. This is because their botanical names will also include the genus, *Poa*, and the species, *pratensis*.

Botanists take plant names one step further by assigning individual plants a third name that shows if they are a variety or cultivar. Varietal plants develop in nature, through natural selection. The varietal name follows the genus and species and is frequently seen italicized after the abbreviation *var.* For example, *Poa pratensis* var. *Park* is another name for Park, one of the original common Kentucky bluegrasses.

With today's push to create improved grasses, you are more apt to come across plants that are cultivars, meaning they were created through deliberate breeding. Cultivar names also follow the genus and species but are enclosed in single quotes and are not italicized or underlined. If you were to see *Poa pratensis* 'America', you would know that you were dealing with a cultivar of Kentucky bluegrass called America.

will do best in the sunny areas. If conditions should turn adverse for one of the grasses, you won't lose the entire lawn, just the part that's made up of the susceptible grass.

Unlike cool-season grasses, warm-season grasses tend to be planted as *monostands*, meaning that a single type of seed is planted, not a mixture. Their growth via stolons and rhizomes makes them so vigorous that other grasses cannot compete. Because of their distinctive appearance, some grasses, such as the original tall fescues and most native grasses, also look better planted alone.

Grass Seed Labels

Thanks to the passage of the Federal Seed Act of 1936, grass-seed labeling must meet certain requirements. This allows you to know at a glance what is in any given box, including what percentage of the seed will germinate. When you shop for seed, it pays to compare brands closely and to remember the adage, "the lawn you grow is no better than the seed you buy." The extra expense for higher-quality seed is usually worth it. Check the labels and try to avoid mixtures containing lower-quality grasses, like timo-

UNDERSTANDING GRASS LABELS

The grasses being bred today have numerous advantages over their older cousins. For starters, many display increased insect and disease resistance and improved drought tolerance.

To reap the benefits such grasses can provide, you'll need to introduce them into your lawn through spot reseeding, lawn renovation, and planting anew. Read the grass-seed label to see whether disease- and pest-resistant cultivars are in a given box of seed.

Blade Type: Fine, narrow-leaved grasses produce attractive and more uniform lawns. Coarse grasses are better for areas that receive hard wear.

Kinds and Percentages (Purity): Package labels must state the name of each kind of seed present and its percentage in the mix. In high-quality seed mixtures, 80 to 100 percent of the total mix will consist of desirable permanent lawn species. The published percentages are based on weight, not the number of seeds. For example, there are approximately 500,000 fine fescue seeds per pound of grass seed and 1 million bluegrass seeds per pound. Thus, in a 50/50 bluegrass/fine fescue mixture measured by weight, only one-third of the total number of seeds is fine fescue, and the bluegrass would predominate with two-thirds of the seeds. (This is desirable because, given their vigorous nature, the fine fescue seedlings would otherwise overwhelm the bluegrass.)

Cultivar: The trade names of the varieties included in the mix and not just the generic names, such as fine fescue,

should be noted on the label. When they aren't, an older variety that may not have the advantages of the new, improved cultivar has probably been used.

Germination: This is the percentage of seeds expected to produce plants under favorable conditions. Look for a minimum germination rate of 75 percent or better for Kentucky bluegrass and at least 85 percent for perennial ryegrass, tall fescue, and fine fescue.

Test Date: This is the date seeds were tested for germination rates. Most states consider germination percentages to be reliable up to nine months after testing. As the seed ages, the germination rate decreases.

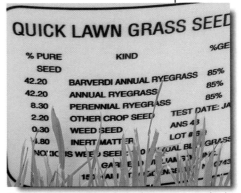

By law, grass seed labels show a great deal of information about seed contents, including germination rates and the date the seeds were tested.

Weed Seeds: Good-quality grass seed usually contains no more than 0.5 percent weed seeds; high-quality grass seed has none.

Noxious Weeds: These are troublesome plant species that are difficult to control. Each state has its own list and amount per pound allowed. Avoid any if possible.

Inert Matter: This is dirt, chaff, and other bits that take up productive seed space. The less, the better.

thy, meadow fescue, orchard grass, tall oatgrass, and annual ryegrass. Look also for endophyte-containing grasses (see below) and for cultivars recommended for your area by your Cooperative Extension Service.

While unused grass seed may remain viable for years, its rate of germination will decrease over time. Be sure to keep seed stored in a cool, dry environment. To maintain optimal viability, the rule of thumb for storage is that the temperature and the relative humidity added together should be less than 100.

Endophytes: Nature's Repellents

Endophytes are small fungi that live in some grasses and make them harmful or deadly to a variety of grass-eating insects. Discovered by scientists in New Zealand who observed that cattle got sick after eating certain grasses, endophytes have opened a new frontier in grass research. Since endophytes live primarily in the lower stem and crown of grass plants, surface pests such as sod webworms, armyworms, billbugs, cutworms and chinch bugs are deterred, but not underground pests like white grubs, which feed on grass roots. Research also suggests that when grasses with endophytes face environmental stresses, such as drought, they fare better than grasses without endophytes.

Endophytic fungi get their start in turf by infecting the grass seed. Harmless to children or pets that may occasionally eat the grass, and to the grass itself, the fungi remain inside the growing plant. New seed produced by infected plants will also contain these important fungi, but unfortunately, it's not currently possible to introduce endophytes separately into established lawns. Ongoing research is focused on finding ways to insert endophytes into different grasses. For now, perennial ryegrasses and fescues are the main species in which endophytes live, and only a limited number of their cultivars have this trait. When buying seed, check to see whether any endophyte

grasses are listed on the label. Endophytes do not stay viable in unused seed for long periods, so keep stored seed cool and plan to use it within nine months of the testing date. The latest information on endophytes will be available from your Cooperative Extension Service. Here are a few of the endophyte-containing cultivars:

Perennial Ryegrass: 'Citation II', 'Repell II', 'Palmer II'
Fine Fescues: 'Jamestown II', 'Reliant'
Tall Fescue: 'Rebel', 'Mustang'

Lawn-Grass Options

See the USDA Plant Hardiness Map on page 54 to find out which zone you live in. The cultivars listed at the end of each description are just a few of those generally recognized to have outstanding characteristics for their species. Are they appropriate choices for your lawn? That depends on the growing environment where you live. Furthermore, with the burgeoning research into new, improved cultivars, change is always on the horizon, so keep up to date by using the suggested resources in Appendix II. (See page 150.)

COOL-SEASON GRASSES

Kentucky bluegrass (*Poa pratensis*)

❑ *Description:* Kentucky bluegrass fills the bill if you want a deep green, fine-textured, attractive lawn. Able to take moisture and temperature extremes, bluegrass is winter hardy and will grow in full sun to light shade depending on cultivar and location. Sown by seed and spread by rhizomes and tillers, it forms strong, dense sod that recovers well from injury. Maintenance requirements vary, with the older common cultivars such as 'Park' and 'Windsor' requiring less water, nutrients, and care, but they are highly susceptible to leaf spot. Newer, more labor-intensive cultivars grow aggressively, crowding out weeds and showing increased resistance to pests and diseases.

Kentucky bluegrass is the most widely used cool-season species and the all-around best choice for general lawn purposes.

Rough-stalked bluegrass likes moist, shady conditions and becomes patchy in sunny areas.

❏ *Drawbacks:* It's slow to germinate, and during prolonged hot dry weather, Kentucky bluegrass goes dormant, losing its color. Performs poorly in wet soils or shade.

❏ *Recommendations:* For USDA Hardiness Zones 2 to 7. When planting a bluegrass lawn, blend at least three varieties to take advantage of differing disease and pest resistances. Generally speaking, look for improved bluegrasses such as 'America', 'Adelphi', 'Glade', and 'Ram I'. 'Glade' and 'Nugget' can tolerate some shade; 'Columbia', 'Adelphi', and 'Parade' are more tolerant of heat and drought.

With more than 100 cultivars to choose from, you're likely to find those suited to your region by consulting a local nursery or your local Cooperative Extension Service.

Rough-stalked bluegrass (*Poa trivialis*)

❏ *Description:* This moderately fine-textured, light-to-medium-green grass spreads by weak stolons. New seedlings are vigorous, tolerating acid soils as well as poorly drained, moist, shaded sites. Not minding low temperatures, rough-stalked bluegrass keeps its color well into the fall. Best in low-traffic areas.

❏ *Drawbacks:* With shallow roots, rough-stalked bluegrass cannot tolerate hot, dry conditions and soon becomes patchy in sunny areas.

❏ *Recommendations:* For USDA Hardiness Zones 4 to 7. Plant in moist shade. Look for the cultivars 'Laser II', 'Colt', and 'Sabre'.

Tall fescue (*Festuca arundinacea*)

❏ *Description:* Having a deep root system that enables it to tolerate drought and heat, tall fescue has been used for years as a durable utility grass. The older, wide-bladed forage types, 'Kentucky 31' and 'Alta', are no longer considered good choices for lawns. Instead choose improved tall fescues known as "turf-type." These denser, finer-leaved, darker turf types have the advantage of being more disease- and insect-resistant.

❏ *Drawbacks:* In far northern regions and areas of shade, tall fescues are prone to thin out and form clumps, causing the lawn to require overseeding. A bunch grass with minimal rhizomes, tall fescue makes a weakish sod that is slow to recover from injury, but the grass itself wears well.

❏ *Recommendations:* For USDA Hardiness Zones 2 to 7. You should stick to the better-looking

Tall fescue is a good choice for sunny lawns and playgrounds in the North and the north-south transitional zone.

turf-types, such as 'Rebel Jr.', 'Monarch', and 'Bonanza II'. These cultivars are often sold in blends.

Fine fescue (*Festuca* species)

❏ *Description:* While genetically different, species in this genus—chewings, creeping red, and hard fescue—share some similar characteristics. They are fine textured and dark green, making them mix well with bluegrasses and perennial rye. Forming a dense, upright, good-looking turf, all grow well in acidic soils and shade. These three are the most drought and shade tolerant of the cool-season grasses, and they don't require much fertilizer. Many fescues are also endophyte-enhanced and, when added to other grasses, increase both their disease and pest resistance. Except for creeping fescue, which has rhizomes, fescues are bunch grasses.

❏ *Drawbacks:* Fescues need well-drained soil and don't stand up well to heat or heavy wear.

❏ *Recommendations:* For USDA Hardiness Zones 2 to 7. Fine fescues are usually found in shade mixtures. Two types of chewings fescue with high endophyte levels are 'Jamestown II' and 'SR 5000'. Other improved insect- and dollar spot-resistant cultivars include 'SR 3000', 'Aurora', 'Biljart', 'Reliant', 'Scaldis', 'Waldina', and 'Spartan'. Sheep fescue is resistant to dollar spot as well.

Perennial ryegrass (*Lolium perenne*)

❏ *Description:* A bright green bunch grass with a fine to medium texture, perennial ryegrass grows well in a wide range of soils, even wet soils. Having finer, denser, darker green leaves, the improved low-growth turf types are replacing older varieties. Many of the new cultivars are also endophyte-enhanced for improved disease- and pest-resistance. Ryegrasses withstand foot traffic and compacted soils. Starting quickly from seed, they make excellent "nurse" grasses, protecting slower-growing species, and are used to overseed warm-season lawns. They do best in coastal regions with mild winters and cool, moist summers.

❏ *Drawbacks:* Perennial ryegrasses, especially older varieties, have a low tolerance for drought and cold and are prone to pythium blight. They are best in mixtures but should not make up more than 20 percent because they grow so vigorously.

❏ *Recommendations:* For USDA Hardiness Zones 3 to 7. Look for new, improved cultivars with endophytes, such as 'Yorktown III' and 'Palmer II'. 'Derby' and 'Pennfine' show good heat and drought tolerance, while 'Regal' displays good cold tolerance.

Fine fescues are ideal for shaded, low-maintenance lawns. They mix well with bluegrasses and perennial ryegrass.

Perennial ryegrass germinates rapidly, wears well, and is frequently found in seed mixtures.

Warm-season St. Augustinegrass here fills the front lawn of the Ernest Hemingway House in Key West, Florida.

St. Augustinegrass is favored in warm, humid climates for its ability to tolerate shade and salt, despite its coarse leaves.

WARM-SEASON GRASSES

St. Augustinegrass (*Stenotaphrum secundatum*)

❏ *Description:* Easily grown from sod, sprigs, or plugs, St. Augustinegrass does well on most moderately fertile soils and produces a dark green to blue-green turf with stolons. While grass blades have a medium-to-coarse texture, seed heads aren't a problem. With proper care, St. Augustine provides a good looking, thick turf in locales where a lack of sun inhibits growth of finer-leaved grasses. This grass grows best in coastal areas from Florida to California.

❏ *Drawbacks:* St. Augustine will lose its color if not kept watered during dry spells, and it's prone to thatch. It doesn't wear well, and certain cultivars are cold sensitive. Viral-induced "St. Augustine decline," which causes the grass to weaken and yellow, is a concern in some areas, and many of its cultivars are attractive to chinch bugs.

❏ *Recommendations:* For USDA Hardiness Zones 8 to 10. Look for improved, chinch bug-resistant varieties like 'Floratam', 'Floralawn', and 'FX-10', which do well in sunny, dry locations. Cultivars 'Bitterblue', 'Jade', and 'Delmar' have greater cold and shade tolerance but less pest resistance.

Bermudagrass (*Cynodon* species)

❏ *Description:* One of the most widely used southern grasses, Bermudagrass thrives on numerous soil types, even salty soils. With a deep root system, it takes sun, heat, and dry conditions in stride, forming a strong, erosion-resistant sod. Having both rhizomes and stolons, Bermudagrass quickly fills in damaged areas with its generally fine, low growth. New hybrids, some growing from seed, show improved color, texture, disease resistance, and cold tolerance. They are less costly to maintain and establish.

Bermudagrass is good for sunny southern lawns that receive heavy use, but it is invasive and so requires edging.

❏ *Drawbacks:* Bermudagrass requires edging to prevent invasive growth; it also forms thatch and generally requires intensive management. Needing full sun, it's the least shade tolerant of southern grasses. It also turns a strawlike brown after a frost, making it a candidate for winter overseeding.

❏ *Recommendations:* For USDA Hardiness Zones 7 to 10. Look for somewhat lower maintenance, improved cultivars, such as 'Guymon', 'Cheyenne', and 'Sundevil'. 'Flora-tex,' available only as sod, is an improved cultivar requiring lower maintenance than the fine-leaved 'Tiflawn', 'Tifgreen II', 'Tifway', and 'Ormond' cultivars.

Zoysiagrass (*Zoysia* species)

❏ *Description:* Popular in the transitional zone and the South, zoysiagrass was once touted as a miracle grass because of its especially thick, slow-growing turf. While it may take two years to establish, you'll end up with a lawn that weeds can rarely penetrate. Having a fine-to-medium texture, its color varies by cultivar. Being deep-rooted and fibrous, it doesn't mind heat or drought, although it does need an occasional watering. Zoysia is winter hardy and isn't particular about soil. It also copes well with salt spray, pests, diseases, and some shade.

❏ *Drawbacks:* The main complaint about zoysia is its unrelenting straw color in the fall. Furthermore, the characteristics that make zoysia so durable also make it prone to thatch and difficult to mow. Add poor recuperative powers and high fertility needs, and you have a high-maintenance turf.

❏ *Recommendations:* For USDA Hardiness Zones 6 to 9. There are several species of zoysia to choose from. *Zoysia japonica*, known as Japanese lawn grass, with its coarse, light green leaves is the best zoysia choice for colder climates. *Zoysia matrella*, also called Manilagrass, is a less winter-hardy, slower-growing species that creates a denser, finer lawn. A preferred *japonica* cultivar, 'Meyer', has deep green leaves. One of the newer japonicas, 'El Toro', looks like 'Meyer' but is said to have better cool-season color, less thatch buildup, and a quicker establishment rate. A hybrid of *Zoysia japonica*, 'Emerald', is perhaps the most attractive cultivar: It has good winter hardiness and color combined with faster growth and fine texture.

Centipedegrass (*Eremochloa ophiuroides*)

❏ *Description:* Growing in full sun to partial shade, this apple green grass prefers well-drained acid soils. It can be grown from seed and is known for

Zoysiagrass provides one of the most uniform and dense lawns possible, but it has a strawlike appearance in winter.

Centipedegrass is a slow-growing option for low-fertility southern lawns, but it doesn't bear up under heavy use.

its slow growth rate, which means it requires less mowing. A low-maintenance warm-season grass, it spreads by stolons, forming a moderately dense low-growth turf of medium-textured grass. With extra fertilizer, it will turn deeper green but becomes more susceptible to cold injury.

❏ *Drawbacks:* Centipedegrass doesn't bear up well under heavy use and is apt to be damaged by nematodes. Salt spray poses problems, as does lack of iron, which leads to yellowing. Avoid using excess amounts of fertilizer, which fosters heavy thatch development that leads to "centipede decline" (large brown dead patches).

❏ *Recommendations:* For USDA Hardiness Zones 7 to 8. Cultivars with better cold tolerance, such as 'Oklawn' and 'Centennial', are available.

Bahiagrass (*Paspalum notatum*)

❏ *Description:* An up-and-comer for low-upkeep home lawns, bahiagrass grows from seed and forms an apple green lawn with a relatively open growth habit. Having gotten its start as a pasture grass on infertile, sandy soils, it has a prolific root system enabling it to withstand drought. It also forms a durable wear-resistant sod, and most pests leave it alone.

❏ *Drawbacks:* Bahiagrass is coarse, making it tough to mow. Some people object to the look of its tall seed heads and light green color. It may yellow from lack of iron and grows poorly in alkaline soils and in areas with salt spray.

❏ *Recommendations:* For USDA Hardiness Zones 7 to 10. Avoid common bahiagrass; 'Argentine' and 'Pensacola' are the preferred cultivars.

Carpetgrass (*Axonopus affinis*)

❏ *Description:* Not minding some shade and preferring wet feet, carpetgrass will grow where few others can. Similar to centipedegrass, with its apple green color and medium-wide blades, carpetgrass is spread by creeping stolons and can be grown from seed. While it won't yield a high-quality lawn, this species provides an alternative for boggy sites in warm climates.

❏ *Drawbacks:* With shallow roots and no rhizomes, carpetgrass needs watering when dry and won't stand up to wear. It's quick to brown-out in the fall and slow to green-up in the spring, and it sends up tall seed heads all summer.

❏ *Recommendations:* For USDA Hardiness Zones 8 to 9. No named varieties are available, so look for the species *Axonopus affinis*.

Bahiagrass grows well in hot climates on infertile, dry soils because of its deep roots, but it is coarse and difficult to mow.

Carpetgrass grows in wet, poorly drained southern soils where other grasses won't.

OVERSEEDING SOUTHERN LAWNS FOR WINTER COLOR

Warm-season grasses have a major drawback for home-owners in need of green vistas: Their color disappears with the onset of winter. To get around this trait, some southerners overseed their lawns using fine fescue, blue-grass, or—the most popular choice—ryegrass. The premise is simple: Cool-season grasses find a hospitable habitat among the dormant southern grasses and then die off with the return of warm weather in the spring. Aside from improved aesthetics, overseeding helps prevent the establishment of winter weeds. The drawback is that overseeding may slow down and even weaken your permanent turf's spring green-up.

Do not overseed until daytime temperatures drop to the low to mid 70s and your permanent lawn grass has gone dormant. To prepare for overseeding, rake off any debris, mow the lawn closely, and dethatch if needed. Ask your local Cooperative Extension Service about cultivars and seeding rates recommended for your area.

Use a spreader to overseed, sowing half in one direction and the other half by walking at right angles to the first. Then, using a stiff broom or rake, go briskly over the lawn to help move the seed down to ground level. Finish off with a light watering and continue to water daily until the seedlings are well established.

Maintaining the grass over the winter will require monthly feeding, along with regular mowing and watering. The temporary winter grass should not be encouraged once spring approaches, so stop fertilizing, water infrequently, and mow closely until the permanent grass resumes growth.

Native Grasses

Having evolved on and adapted to the arid grassland plains, these grasses are survivors. They require little maintenance and provide a grass cover that is more open and natural in appearance than traditional turf grasses. Native grasses grow best during the hot summer months and prefer full sun. They are widely adapted to areas across the United States and Canada and are especially suited to the grasslands of the Central Plains states. Check with your local Cooperative Extension Service to learn whether natives are suitable for your region.

Buffalograss (Buchloe dactyloides)

Coming from the Great Plains where water efficiency is a necessity, buffalograss is resistant to both heat and drought. It tolerates cool temperatures better than most warm-season grasses and keeps its color into the fall. Often grown from seed, it spreads slowly by stolons and self-sown seeds to form a gray-green, fine-textured lawn that attains a height of 4 to 5 inches. Best in full sun, it prefers well-drained loam and abhors wet, poorly drained, or sandy soils. Depending on rainfall, it may still need an occasional watering to prevent summer dormancy, but far less than other grasses. Because it grows slowly, buffalograss needs only several mowings a season. Its sparse appearance is not for everyone, and it doesn't do as well in humid regions, such as Florida. It has few pest

Buffalograss thrives in hot, dry climates and only occasionally needs watering or mowing. It rarely needs fertilizing, and few pests feed on it.

Blue grama is a tough grass that wears well under heavy use and tolerates heat, drought, and cold. Like buffalograss, it requires little mowing.

As with all prairie grasses, crested wheatgrass requires little upkeep. It thrives in cool, semi-arid conditions and needs few waterings because of its deep root system.

problems, but white grubs, webworms, and chinch bugs do feed on it. When buying, look for improved cultivars, such as '609', 'Plains', '315', 'Prairie', 'Cody', and 'Topgun'.

Blue grama (*Bouteloua gracilis*)

Blue grama grows well from seed and forms a gray-green, low-growth turf that spreads slowly by rhizomes. Having a fibrous root system, it forms strong sod and is quite tolerant of heat and drought, although it will turn brown and go dormant. It tolerates low temperatures but is slow to green-up in the spring. It's better adapted to both sandy and fine soils than buffalograss because it tolerates alkaline conditions. In arid areas, blue grama is frequently mixed with buffalograss for a low-maintenance lawn that needs little mowing. Its seed heads and small flowers make it an interesting choice for naturalistic areas.

Crested wheatgrass (*Agropyron cristatum*)

Frequently used along roadways and for lawns planted on dry lands, this hardy cool-season bunch grass produces long, coarse, medium-green tapered foliage that is well adapted to cool, semi-arid conditions. In states such as Wyoming, where yearly rainfall may range from 8 to 15 inches, crested wheatgrass thrives, thanks to its especially deep root system. It develops flat, cockscomb-like seed heads and will become partially dormant during hot spells. As with other prairie grasses, it doesn't require much mowing or other upkeep. 'Fairway' is the preferred cultivar—it is leafier and finer textured than common crested wheatgrass.

chapter 6

Steps for Restoring a Lawn

A RESTORATION ALLOWS YOU to improve your lawn without removing the existing turf. You'll have the best chance of success if your lawn scored more than 15 points on the score sheet on page 16. While restoring your lawn is not nearly as labor intensive as removing all of your turf and starting over, it will still require several weekends of work. In this chapter, each step of a lawn restoration is described, some of which are essential and others optional. In most parts of North America, the best time to begin restoration is late summer or fall, although adjusting pH and dethatching can be done in the spring to prepare for a fall restoration. You will see some improvement in a restored lawn during the season in which you begin, but you will need two or three growing seasons to see dramatic progress.

Restoring a Lawn

STEP One

Remove thatch and weeds. When beginning a lawn restoration, the first step is to remove any thatch buildup—even low levels that would otherwise be acceptable. Unless you can expose the soil between the old grass plants, the steps that follow will have poor results. While you're at it, make a note of weed colonies and remove the worst of them with a grape (grubbing) hoe before proceeding to Step 2.

The best time to dethatch is when your lawn is thriving—not when it's stressed in the heat of summer or cold of

winter. To begin, set the height adjustment on your mower to cut the grass about 1 inch high, essentially half its normal mowing height. Mow the entire lawn. Short grass will make dethatching and surface preparation easier. It will also improve seed germination rates because more seed will make contact with the soil and seedlings will have greater exposure to the sun.

The easiest way to remove thatch from a lawn that is more than 3,000 square feet is with a power rake, or vertical mower (a machine with vertical instead of horizontal cutting blades), which should be available at rental stores. For smaller lawns or lawns with thin, ½- to 1-inch layers of thatch, a manual thatching rake will do a satisfactory job.

When using a vertical mower to remove average amounts of thatch and to scarify the soil, set the blades to cut ⅛ to ¼ inch into the soil. Make several test passes on an inconspicuous area of your lawn to judge how much thatch (and turf) will be removed. If too much or too little is removed, raise or lower the blades accordingly. The spacing between blades can be adjusted on some machines, but this is difficult to do and so is best done by the rental store staff. The blade spacing for Bermudagrass and zoysiagrass is 1 to 2 inches, while the spacing for bahiagrass and St. Augustinegrass is 3 inches. Most rental store owners will know the optimal settings for the grasses grown in your area.

When using a vertical mower to dethatch, make several passes over the lawn in perpendicular directions. It is important to be thorough. Remove the thatch you pull up after each series of passes and add it to your compost pile. When you have finished dethatching, remow your lawn to a height of 1 inch. For more information on manual thatching rakes, power rakes, and vertical mowers, see "Appendix I," page 142.

On a lawn with thick thatch (more than 1½ inches), you may need to partially remove the thatch and allow the lawn to fully recover before the next dethatching

Left Use a thatching rake, as shown. Angle the head so that its sharp tines slightly cut into the ground. Use a push-pull stroke to lift the thatch. **Inset** If you have large lawn areas with thatch, consider renting a power rake, sometimes called a vertical mower.

session. Removing too much thatch all at once can do more harm than good. The rule of thumb is to remove what you can without tearing up holes of more than a couple of square inches in live turf. This may not be possible on lawns with very thick thatch—more than 2 inches. In that case, your lawn may not be salvageable and may need to be replanted from scratch. (See Chapter 7, "Starting a New Lawn from Scratch," page 76.)

STEP TWO

Fill depressions and level bumps. While you are dethatching your lawn, check for bumps and depressions. These may have been caused by poor grading, uneven settling, or the decomposition of buried tree stumps, logs, or roots. Mark any irregularities with latex spray paint so that you can find them easily when you are ready to level them.

To level small bumps, raise the sod with a sharp spade and remove the necessary amount of soil beneath it. Cut out at least a 2x2-foot section of sod. If you lift smaller patches of sod, they will likely dry out and die. While the soil base is exposed, mix in some compost and fertilizer. Watersoak the area using a hose and press the sod back into place. Keep the area watered to prevent lawn brownout.

Slight depressions can be smoothed over by top-dressing: applying to the surface topsoil a combination of topsoil and compost. A wide landscaping rake is the best tool for this job. When handling larger depressions—those more than an inch or two deep and several square feet in area—raise the sod; fill the depression with a mixture of soil, humus, and fertilizer; replace the sod; and press it in place. Be sure to keep repaired areas moist, or the edges will dry out and turn brown.

FILLING A DEPRESSION

1 Use a spade to cut turf around the depression on three sides. Then roll back the turf.

2 With the turf rolled back, fill the depression with a mixture of soil, compost, and fertilizer.

3 Roll the sod back into place.

4 Sift soil into the seams, tamp lightly, and water thoroughly.

STEP Three

Adjust your soil's pH. Before applying anything, it is best to test your own soil or obtain test results from a professional testing service. If your soil test shows that the soil pH is low, add lime according to the test recommendations. If you did your own pH test and thus have no recommendations to go by, use the table below, "Amounts of CCE-Rated Finely Ground Limestone Required to Raise pH," to determine how much lime to apply. If you're unsure of your test results, be conservative. Too much of an amendment can be as detrimental to your lawn as none at all.

Lime amendments come in various forms, from ground oyster shells to liquids. Agricultural ground limestone is the preferred type because it is readily available and can be safely, easily, and accurately applied with a drop or rotary spreader. (See page 144.)

To minimize dust and ensure uniform application when applying lime to acid soils, use a pelletized lime. This is a finely ground limestone that has been mixed with a soluble binder to form pellets; in the photos it is being applied with a drop spreader.

There are two types of agricultural ground limestone: dolomitic and calcitic. Both contain calcium carbonate, a grass nutrient, and a neutralizer for acidic soil. Dolomitic limestone contains magnesium, another important nutrient, as well as calcium carbonate. Use dolomitic limestone if your soil is deficient in magnesium. Calcitic limestone does not contain magnesium, making it more appropriate if your soil is already high in magnesium. However, adding dolomitic limestone to soil already high in magnesium has not been shown to cause lawn problems.

For faster results, choose a finely ground limestone. Fine grinds begin to correct the soil pH faster than coarse grinds. Coarsely ground limestone acts

Amounts of CCE-Rated Finely Ground Limestone Required to Raise pH
(in pounds per 1,000 square feet)

pH Adjustment	Fescues		Kentucky Blue, Bermuda, Rye	
	Sands & Sandy Loams	Loams & Clays	Sands & Sandy Loams	Loams & Clays
5.8–6.2 to 6.5	0	0	25	35
5.3–5.7 to 6.5	25	35	50	75
4.8–5.2 to 6.5	50	75	75	100
4.0–4.7 to 6.5	75	100	100	100

Note: Do not add lime if your pH is 6.3 or higher.

slowly and is better suited for use once you have raised your pH to a desirable range. You can tell fine lime from coarse if you understand the information on the package. The higher the percentage of ground lime that passes through the finer sieves, the finer the grind. Sieves are graded by number; the higher the number, the smaller the sieve holes. Look for a product stating that 50 percent or more of the ground limestone will pass through a Number 100 sieve. *Caution*: Fine grinds can burn grass. Check instructions on the packaging.

One more thing to keep in mind when buying lime is its relative purity. Liming materials are rated according to their Calcium Carbonate Equivalent (CCE). A CCE rating of 100 is equal to pure calcium carbonate; less than 100 indicates less neutralizing ability than calcium carbonate. Account for the CCE when figuring how much lime to apply to your lawn. If the CCE of the product you purchase is 80 and your soil test recommendations assume a CCE of 100, you will need to increase the recommended application rate by 20 percent.

As shown in the table on the previous page, the more clay and organic content in your soil, the more lime you will need to correct the pH. Sandy soils require less lime to raise pH. If you need to add more than 40 pounds of lime per 1,000 square feet to correct your pH, do it in two or more applications. And don't apply lime with fertilizer mixed in the same spreader. The resulting chemical reaction will release the nitrogen you want for your grass into the air. After spreading lime, water the lawn to wash the particles off the grass leaves and into the soil.

To lower the pH, add sulfur according to your soil test recommendations. Sulfur amendments are also available in the form of compounds, such as ammonium sulfate. These compounds can be used in place of elemental sulfur, but they can burn turf if used in excess. See amendment packaging for details on amounts that can be safely applied to turfgrass.

If you are relying on your own test kit and not a professional test, follow the recommendations in the table below. Sulfur acts within one month to lower soil pH. To avoid applying too much, don't try to make your correction in one application. To meet recommended amounts, make several surface applications a few weeks apart and water the grass after each application.

STEP Four

Add nutrients. When restoring a lawn, apply the fertilizer recommended by the results of your soil test. Use a slow-release fertilizer, and avoid putting down more fertilizer than you need. Adding too much nitrogen can cause rapid growth and a thinning of plant cell walls, which makes grass more susceptible to disease. The excess fertilizer may also leach and eventually find its way into waterways, polluting them.

Amounts of Elemental Sulfur Required to Lower pH (in pounds per 1,000 square feet)			
pH Adjustment	Loam	Sandy Soil	Clay Soil
7.5 to 6.5	18	12	23
8 to 6.5	34	28	46
8.5 to 6.5	57	46	69

To add nutrients, use a slow-release fertilizer that keeps applications to a minimum. *Inset* Set the spreader to deliver half the amount of fertilizer recommended by your soil test.

If you did not test your soil, apply a slow-release fertilizer with a Nitrogen-Phosphorus-Potassium ratio of 3-1-2. Apply about ½ pound of nitrogen per 1,000 square feet of lawn. (See "Turf Fertilization," page 100, for more on fertilizer types.)

STEP Five

Build organic matter and microbe numbers.
The right dose of fertilizer won't help much if your soil does not contain an adequate population of microbes; you need billions of these microscopic organisms per handful. Microbes not only digest grass clippings, dead grass roots, and old stems, but they also make their nutrients available to living grass plants.

To have a thriving microbe population your soil must contain 2 to 5 percent organic material. A topdressing of compost mixed with topsoil followed by aeration will eventually incorporate some organic matter into the soil without disrupting the lawn.

When topdressing your lawn, apply about 1 cubic yard, which is 100 pounds of a 40-60 mix of topsoil and compost, per 1,000 square feet. Topsoil is available from most nurseries and landscape centers. Be sure it has a dark, rich, brown color and that it has not been diluted with lighter-colored subsoils. Compost can be obtained from several sources. Many towns make compost available to residents at little or no cost. They make compost from the leaves, grass, and brush that residents haul to the dump. The compost should

APPLYING ORGANIC MATTER

To spread a compost-soil topdressing, work the material together in a wheelbarrow and dump piles at regular intervals.

Spread the compost-soil mixture evenly with a wide rake and work it down to the roots of the grass.

be screened to ¼- or ⅜-inch particles, and it should be free of inorganic materials, such as shreds of plastic leaf bags. Its moisture content should be 30 to 50 percent. Any drier, and the compost releases a lot of dust as it's being worked; any wetter, and the material tends to clump and not mix well with soil. Compost is also available from nurseries and landscape centers. Better yet, make your own. For more on compost, see "Making Compost," page 32.

STEP Six

Aerate compacted lawns. Aeration, also called core cultivation or aerifying, is an important part of any lawn restoration program. It allows grass roots to deeply penetrate the soil, helps fertilizer and organic matter get to the roots, allows oxygen to reach the roots, and makes it easier for water to soak into the soil. Simply aerate once in the fall. Avoid aerating during dry summer months because you may damage an already stressed lawn. Also, avoid periods when weed seeds are prevalent, as that could cause weed infestation.

There are several types of aerating tools. Manual aerators allow you to do small areas a little at a time and to aerate corners and other tight areas difficult to reach with large equipment. You supply the power for these tools by pushing the hollow cylinders or corers into the turf—much as you would push in a spade. The tool cuts a plug, or core, that is extracted and deposited on the lawn the next time you push it into the turf. Small power aerators work

AERATING COMPACTED SOIL

Above left This aerator operates best when tilted forward so that its weight pushes the corers into the soil. *Above right* These cores were extracted by the rotary aerator (shown). *Above* Resembling long, slim scoopers, corers like the one in this closeup extract plugs from the soil's top layer and deposit them on the surface.

A manual aerator does an excellent job but much more slowly.

similarly and are available at rental stores. Some machines use a rotating, tillerlike action that pushes the corers into the soil and extracts small plugs, as the machines pull you forward. These lawn mower-size machines will fit into a full-size station wagon, minivan, or pickup truck, and they require two people to transport them.

Avoid aerators that only poke holes in the lawn without removing plugs because they are of less value to your lawn. The largest aerators require a truck and several helpers to transport them but do a better job. With these machines, the corers are vertically plunged into the turf to extract a sizable plug. You may opt to have a pro tackle this job.

Aerators penetrate your lawn best when the soil has been moistened by rain or watering. So unless it rains, water your lawn the day before aerating. When aerating, make several passes in several directions over every square foot of lawn. Next, break up all the plugs extracted by the aerator with the back of a rake or by dragging a metal mesh doormat or section of chain link fence over the plugs to spread the soil. You can also mix the soil from the plugs with the topdressing you added in Step 5. Then water thoroughly.

STEP Seven

Prepare the surface and overseed it. In the North, the best time to overseed is in late summer and early fall, although you may also try this technique in early spring. Starting then gives the young grass plants a better chance to germinate, establish strong roots,

OVERSEEDING BARE PATCHES

1 To repair the bare patch shown at center right, loosen the soil to a depth of 6 to 8 inches.

2 Level the soil using a garden rake, and remove all debris.

3 Evenly spread a mixture of fertilizer, seed, and soil over the affected areas.

4 To firm the reseeded area, tamp it with a flat surface, or roll it with a one-third full roller.

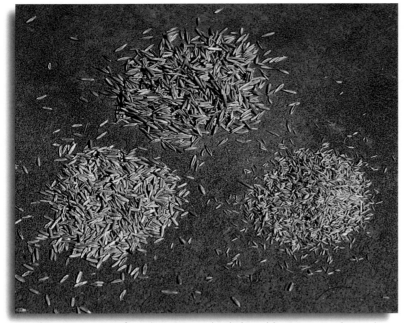

Seed types vary significantly in size. Check the table "How Much Seed to Use When Overseeding" (below) and manufacturers' recommendations for application rates for new and overseeded lawns.

You have several tool options for spreading seed evenly and at the recommended rates. They include your own hands, handheld and walk-behind spreaders, and slit-seeders, which are power machines that cut shallow slits in the soil and sow seed at the same time. Available at many rental stores, slit-seeders are the preferred tool, especially if you were not able to remove all thatch prior to overseeding. (See "Appendix I," page 142, for more details on these tools.)

If you will be spreading seed by hand or with a spreader, first use a thatching rake to roughen the exposed soil to a depth of ½ inch. Set the spreader to deliver the seed that's recommended by the seed producer for seeding a new lawn, or see the table below. If you were not able to remove all thatch, sow a little extra seed. Similarly, the higher the percentage of weeds in your lawn, the more seed you should sow. For sowing grass seed, the recommended approach is to apply seed to the edges of the area you are sowing first. Then divide your seed and apply half while walking in one direction, the other half while walking in a perpendicular direction. Spread extra seed on bare areas, and lightly cover the seed with a mixture of compost and topsoil. Then spread more seed on top.

Finally, follow up by rolling all seeded areas with a water-weighted roller that is one-third full to press the seed into the soil. These steps will help prevent the seed from drying out rapidly and will consequently improve germination rates.

and store food needed for a head start in the spring. In the South, the recommended time to overseed is spring or early summer.

Before you begin, choose the seed that's best for you based on the information in Chapter 5, "Choosing the Right Grass," beginning on page 50. Be sure to select one of the new varieties bred to withstand the stresses your lawn faces. Then use the table "How Much Seed to Use When Overseeding" to help you estimate how much seed to buy.

How Much Seed to Use When Overseeding				
Seed Type	Bluegrass	Tall Fescue	Perennial Ryegrass	Fine Fescue
Pounds per 1,000 square feet	1-2*	4*	4*	2*

*Some experts recommend exceeding these amounts.

If you have a lawn with grass that spreads by stolons (aboveground runners), such as Bermudagrass, St. Augustine, zoysia, or buffalograss, you may introduce new grass plants by inserting plugs rather than seed. (See "Plugging," page 88.)

STEP Eight

Take care of young plants. Your work to this point will have been in vain if you don't care for the young grass plants as the seeds germinate and begin to grow. The most critical need is to apply water at least twice a day, assuming no rain. If the soil is allowed to dry out, the seedlings won't germinate or will soon wither and die. To maximize the germination rate, soak your lawn on the same day you sow the seeds. On the next day, assuming no rain, lightly sprinkle or mist the lawn for about five minutes morning and afternoon. Be sure you have moistened the soil to a depth of 1 inch. Keep the overseeded lawn moist until the young grass plants are 2 inches tall by repeating a light watering every day after periods without rain. This will take four to six weeks. When the grass is 2 inches tall, resume normal watering patterns. For tips on setting up a convenient, low-cost irrigation system, see page 96.

If the weather is dry or warm, spread a layer of straw mulch to protect the seed from the drying effects of sun and wind. Use clean mulching straw that's free of seed. Evenly spread about 100 pounds per 1,000 square feet. Avoid putting down a heavy layer that would inhibit grass growth.

Begin mowing once the grass reaches 2 inches. Use a sharp blade; a dull one may tear up young grass plants. Otherwise, stay off the seeded areas, except to fertilize once more. If needed, apply a second dose of ½ pound of nitrogen per 1,000 square feet six weeks after germination.

From a tiny seed, a young grass plant emerges. From planting through this period, water at least twice a day.

Keep young grass plants moist. Resume normal watering patterns when grass height reaches 2 inches.

chapter 7

Starting a New Lawn from Scratch

F YOUR LAWN SUFFERS FROM acute soil compaction, rampant weed problems, heavy thatch, or nutrient and organic matter deficiencies, you may want to remove your existing turf and replant your lawn. That's a big job, but like a new roof, your new lawn will last a long time. There are four ways to replant a lawn: by applying seed, planting either sprigs or plugs, or laying sod.

❏ Seeds are applied to a new lawn as discussed in the previous chapter, except that they are applied to soil from which all the turf has been removed.

❏ Sprigs are typically planted by machine over large lawns; in small areas, they can be planted by hand. Sprigs consist of cut-up lengths of underground or aboveground runners, called rhizomes or stolons, upon which there are typically two to four joints, or nodes, from which the new grass blades emerge. Sprigs can be broadcast and then pressed into the soil or planted in shallow furrows.

❏ Plugs—round or square pieces of sod that measure about 2 inches across—are planted in holes that are evenly spaced throughout the lawn. After several months, the grass plants from the plugs spread and fill in the gaps.

❑ Sod is available in carpetlike sheets that are usually ¾ inch thick, 1½ feet wide, and about 6 feet long. Pieces should be laid perpendicular to a slope in a staggered pattern, as you would lay bricks.

Comparing the Four Methods

Seeding, a job that even beginners can tackle, is the least expensive planting option. Seeding requires less work than the other planting methods but longer-term care. In most regions, except the South, the best time to seed cool-season grasses is in late summer or early fall, when upper soil mean temperatures are 68° to 86°F. This will allow your new turf to establish roots before the dormant winter period begins, while plant growth is vigorous and competition from weeds is low. Grass plants started in the fall will have a strong start in the spring and a root system sturdy enough to survive the following summer's hot, dry weather. In the South, spring and summer seeding are recommended for warm-season grasses (such as bahiagrass, centipedegrass, carpetgrass, and buffalograss). The temperature of the upper soil should be 68° to 95°F. Check with your Cooperative Extension Service for recommended timing in your area.

Sprigging and plugging are methods typically reserved for warm-season grasses for which seed is not readily available, such as improved strains of Bermudagrass, zoysia, and St. Augustinegrass. Sprigging is best done during the height of the growing season, in spring and summer. Avoid planting when most weeds germinate (spring in the North and fall in the South). It's feasible to plant small areas by either sprigs or plugs. Plugging is generally a more reliable way to generate a new lawn than sprigging, but sprigging is easier to do, and once rooted, sprigs will knit together faster to form

Left A homeowner rolls newly sown seed to press it into the soil. Other options for starting a lawn include laying sod (*middle inset*) and plugs (*top inset*).

turf. In general, sprigs take less time to grow turf than plugs do. Depending on the spacing and type of grass used, it takes several months to grow turf from sprigs and six months or more from plugs.

Sod requires more skill to plant, but it's okay to try your luck with small lawns or lawn sections. Sod offers several advantages over seed, plugs, or sprigs. It looks good immediately, and sodded lawns can be used much sooner than lawns planted by the other methods.

Sod is better than seed for planting on sloping terrain, where seed would be washed to low areas after the first hard rain. In addition, sod is less susceptible to erosion while it is becoming established and makes it harder for weeds to compete. Sodding is best done in the fall or spring in the North and in the spring in the South. Plant the sod during cool, humid weather, because planting it in warm, dry weather will subject it to burnout. Do not plant sod later than one month before the first fall frost, because you want to give the grass time to establish roots before cold weather sets in.

Preparation for a New Lawn

Planting a new lawn is a big job. You may want to tackle this in sections. Begin by redoing the worst or most visible lawn areas; then make plans to tackle other areas the following year. This keeps the job manageable and makes the critical step of watering more feasible for homeowners who do not have in-ground sprinkler systems. If you don't already have an in-ground system, the approaches described in this book should eliminate the need for one. You will need to take the following steps no matter which grass-planting method you choose.

STEP One
Remove the old turf. There are several ways to kill and remove poor-quality turf. For areas where you don't mind a little temporary unsightliness, solarization or heavy mulching are two methods to consider. Solarization bakes grass and weeds to death

Spread plastic over areas to be replanted and let heat kill off old turf. Seal the edges of the plastic with boards or soil.

under a layer of clear plastic that's anchored over the lawn. You'll need two months to achieve the desired effect, provided you install the plastic when the weather is warm. Don't attempt solarization in shady areas or if your summer nights are cool. Smothering ragged turf with heavy mulches, such as old carpeting, 6 inches of wood chips, or several layers of newspaper covered by 3 inches of wood chips, will have the same effect.

Although not a method we recommend, you may choose to use an herbicide to kill unwanted grass and weeds to the roots. Select an herbicide that degrades quickly (that does not last long in the environment), such as glyphosate (Roundup). Mix according to the manufacturer's directions, and completely cover all grass plants and weeds with the solution. Work on a windless day when the temperature is above 60°F, and take care not to overspray on garden plants. Glyphosate is a potent, nonselective herbicide that will kill or severely injure all foliage it touches. Wear clothing that covers your skin completely, as well as eye protection, when applying this or any other herbicide. Afterwards, take a shower and wash clothing according to precautions on page 128.

You may find that it takes two applications of glyphosate to get the job done. If the turf has not completely died after four weeks, reapply the herbicide and wait seven days after the last application before tilling the dead turf into your soil. Take care to follow the manufacturer's safety precautions.

Mechanical (manual or power) removal of undesirable turf is the fastest way to get the job done without needing to worry about kids or pets contacting herbicides or tracking them into your house. For small lawns, a grape (grubbing) hoe

is a terrific tool for removing turf. Anyone with a strong back and a helper to cart away the old turf pieces can remove up to 300 square feet in an hour. For large lawns, consider renting a sod cutter. It slices under the grass, enabling you to pull up strips of old turf. Make the job easier by cutting sod while the lawn soil is moist. Follow up with tilling to alleviate compaction and to prepare the soil for the amendments you'll mix in later.

Another method of turf removal, turning existing turf into the soil with a tiller or cultivator, is

REMOVING OLD TURF

1 Remove old lawn after a heavy rain or deep watering. First, make 2-inch-deep cuts in the turf every 2 feet.

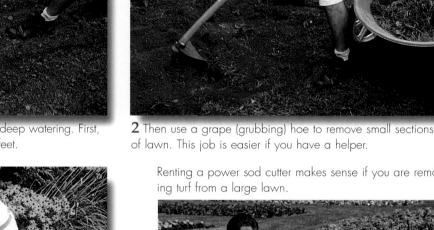

2 Then use a grape (grubbing) hoe to remove small sections of lawn. This job is easier if you have a helper.

Renting a power sod cutter makes sense if you are removing turf from a large lawn.

3 The idea is to skim the grass just below the grade. Let the weight of the tool do the work of chipping away at the grass.

not recommended. Only the most heavy-duty tillers are suited for "busting sod." And raking out the pieces of turf after they've been turned under is frustratingly difficult.

STEP Two

Fix grade problems. Before adding amendments to the soil, fix any existing grade problems. Although grading often requires help from a landscaping contractor with heavy equipment, minor problems can be fixed by the ambitious do-it-yourselfer. Small versions of earth-moving equipment are often available for rent.

The first rule of grading is that the ground should slope away from your house in all directions so that it drops at least 2 or 3 inches every 10 feet. The finished grade should also end up matching the level of existing fixtures, such as permanent walks and patios, as well as areas of lawn that are not being replanted.

This takes some figuring. If you will be replanting with seed and adding 1 inch of amendments, grade so that the level is 1 inch lower than fixtures. If you will be replanting with sod and adding an inch of amendments, the grade should be about 2 inches lower than your fixtures. Your goal is to have the finished grade—after the sod has been planted and amendments added—even with the level of your fixtures.

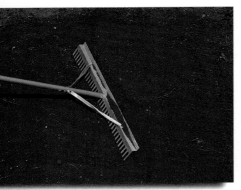

For making minor grade adjustments, a landscape rake is the tool of choice.

Water the area and check for puddles. When the ground has dried adequately, fill where puddles formed using soil from high spots.

The proper way to regrade is first to remove the topsoil from the problem area. Make adjustments to the subsoil by scraping away high areas and filling in low areas. Then spread 2 inches of the reserved topsoil over the subsoil, and till it into the first 2 inches of subsoil. This will help prevent drainage problems between the two layers of soil. Lastly, spread the rest of your topsoil, which should make up at least another 4 inches. If you need to add topsoil, buy a loam that's free of debris, such as roots or stones. It should also be free of weed seeds and pesticides. A landscaping rake is the best tool for working topsoil to the proper grade if you're doing it yourself.

The maximum slope in a lawn should be 12 inches for every 4 feet. If the drop is greater than 12 inches, you should plan to build a low retaining wall or cover the slope with a hardy ground cover or ornamental grass. For further guidance on such grading, see "Solve Poor Drainage," page 47.

STEP Three

Amend the soil. Don't put away or return the tiller yet. Now is your chance to add amendments such as fertilizer, organic matter, and lime or sulfur. The opportunity probably won't come again, so don't skimp. The right way to proceed is to add recommended amendments according to the results of your soil test. To have your soil tested, send

Once the grade is set, evenly spread amendments, such as composted manure, using a garden rake.

Use a tiller to work amendments, including fertilizer, lime, and organic matter, into the soil.

STEP Four

Rake smooth and firm. Rake the area to be replanted until it's smooth. Remove any stones and vegetative matter brought to the surface during tilling. Once you're satisfied, water the ground and check it for puddles. When the soil is dry enough to be worked, move soil from high spots to fill the depressions.

Whether you're planting seed, sprigs, plugs, or sod, it is helpful to roll the prepared soil to provide a firmer base on which to work and to foster adequate soil structure. For example, seed planted in soil that is too loose generally ends up being planted too deeply. The tiny plants may die before they reach the surface. Fill a lawn roller about one-third full of water for this job, and roll the soil until your footprints are no deeper than ½ inch. Complete planting preparations by watering the area thoroughly two days before planting. Check to be sure the soil is moistened to a depth of at least 5 or 6 inches.

samples to the local Cooperative Extension Service or a commercial soil testing lab. The typical recommendations for every 1,000 square feet of new lawn include about 2 pounds of actual (elemental) phosphorus and potassium; 50 to 100 pounds of lime (in areas with acid soil), and 3 to 6 cubic yards of organic matter (such as compost or peat moss) per 1,000 square feet. Recommendations will vary depending on your soil's nutrient, organic matter, and pH levels and on your particular soil type. To be sure, consult with your Cooperative Extension Service.

Ensure an even application of amendments by dividing the recommended amounts in half and applying half while walking in one direction and the other half while walking in a perpendicular direction. Once you have applied the amendments, till them into the top 6 inches of soil.

If an overabundance of weeds was one of your reasons for redoing this section of lawn, allow the many weed seeds in the turned soil to sprout. If you rake through or till under the weed seedlings, you can eliminate most annual weeds.

Use a garden rake to remove stones and debris, as shown below. Then level with a landscape rake, as shown at right.

Choose a Planting Option

Once you've chosen a lawn-planting option, whether it's sodding, seeding, sprigging, or plugging, you should proceed according to the following guidelines.

Preparing Soil and Laying Sod

Before you begin, apply a starter fertilizer high in phosphorus (such as a 2-1-1 or 1-1-1 ratio). Then lightly water the area where you will be installing the sod. Be prepared to begin work when your order is delivered. Sod can go bad quickly, especially if it begins to heat up or dry out. Have the pallets delivered to a shady spot. If you can't start right away, unroll the sod and keep it moist.

Lay sod over one section of lawn at a time. Begin by laying full strips along the outside edge (such as the sidewalk) of the area you plan to sod. Starting with a straight row will reduce the amount of cutting and fitting you'll do later. Next, work toward the opposite edge of lawn, usually the edge by your house. Use a sharp blade to cut as required. Make your last row a full-width strip, if possible. With contoured or irregular borders, lay the strips so that they overlap the border; trim away the excess later.

Prepare soil for sod by rolling with a one-third full roller.

Most rollers are filled at a hole in the side of the drum and plugged with a rubber stopper that expands when tightened.

Reject sod with rips or holes.

The rolled soil should be compacted enough so that your footprints are no deeper than ½ inch.

Lightly water the area to be sodded.

To cut sod, use any sharp knife. Some pros make a handy sod cutter by sharpening the edge of a mason's trowel.

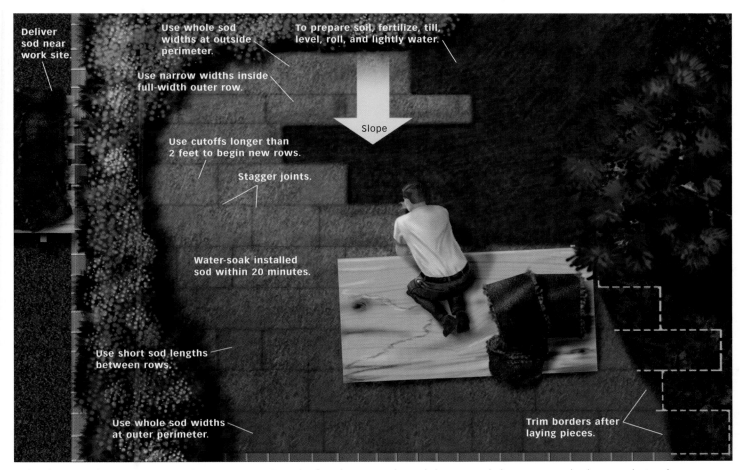

Deliver sod near work site.

Use whole sod widths at outside perimeter.

To prepare soil, fertilize, till, level, roll, and lightly water.

Use narrow widths inside full-width outer row.

Slope

Use cutoffs longer than 2 feet to begin new rows.

Stagger joints.

Water-soak installed sod within 20 minutes.

Use short sod lengths between rows.

Use whole sod widths at outer perimeter.

Trim borders after laying pieces.

When laying sod, start at your outer lawn perimeter. Fit ends of each strip snugly, and do not stretch the strips to make them reach. Lay the next row against the first, staggering ends to prevent water runoff from eroding soil from joints. Kneel to the sodded side of each row, and use a broad board to distribute your weight and to prevent damage to sod. Do not walk or kneel on the prepared soil. Save cutoff ends for the next row. If they are at least 2 feet long, use them as starters. Use shorter cutoffs inside the row, not at the ends. Trim away excess at bed contours with an edger.

LAYING SOD

1 Use a sharpened trowel to make it easy to cut sod to fit at butt joints (shown) or when cutting against a straightedge.

2 You may also use the trowel to level any minor irregularities in the soil while laying the sod.

3 As you lay the sod, keep all joints as tight as possible, but avoid overlapping or stretching the sod.

4 After you have installed each piece of sod, apply water until the sod is completely soaked. This requires about 1 inch of water.

5 When fitting two pieces of sod at an odd angle, try laying one piece over the other and cutting through both at once. Then lift the top piece and remove the waste below.

6 When you have laid sod to the opposite side of the area you're working in, cut the next to last piece to fit. To do this, roll out the sod for a careful test fit.

7 Then, using a long board as a straightedge, make your cut. Discard the piece of waste sod that remains.

8 It's important to have full strips at the perimeter. These are the strips most likely to dry out. They will dry out more quickly if narrow.

9 Where needed, use edger to trim bed.

10 Use a roller to eliminate air pockets under newly laid sod.

11 Fill the joints between sod strips with fine soil.

12 Use a rake to work soil into small cracks.

Along a curved border, let the strips overlap the border.

Then trim the excess sod as close to the border as possible.

To secure sod on a slope, drive stakes through it.

Again, try to install all the sod the day it's delivered. If you have sod left over, unroll it in a shady spot, water it lightly, and use it the next day. If you do sod your lawn in sections, you will need to lay sod against part of the existing lawn. You may find it helpful to use twine and stakes to mark the dividing line. Use the twine as a guide to cut a straight line in the existing turf with a manual or power edger. Lay sod to this edge and try to make a tight, unobtrusive seam. If you're installing sod on a slope, start laying the sod at the lowest point. Stake each piece in three places to prevent slippage. Stakes should be equally spaced and set in from the sod strip's edges by at least 6 to 8 inches.

After installing the sod, firm it by rolling with a one-third full roller. If the roller is too heavy, it could cause the sod to slip. In hot weather, lightly watering the sod prior to rolling will also help prevent slippage. Follow rolling immediately with a thorough soaking—to a depth of 6 to 8 inches.

Seeding

Apply a starter fertilizer (one with a nutrient ratio of 1–1–1 or 1–2–1) to the prepared surface, but do not till it in. Then spread the best seed you can afford at the rate recommended by the seed packager, usually given in pounds per 1,000 square feet.

CONSUMER TIPS FOR BUYING SOD

❏ Buy certified products only.

❏ Examine sod carefully for weeds, disease, and insects, as well as for undesirable grass varieties mixed into the ones specified.

❏ Test sod for handling ease by lifting a 4-foot strip.

If it falls apart, it will be hard to handle at the site.

❏ If the sod has rents or holes, it may have been grown on uneven terrain. Reject the affected pieces.

❏ If the sod is greenish yellow, bluish green, or dry, don't accept it.

How Much Seed to Use for New Lawns				
Seed Type	Kentucky Bluegrass	Tall Fescue	Perennial Ryegrass	Fine Fescue
Pounds per 1,000 square feet	2-3	5–7	4-6	4

Note: Setter spreadings vary with type and model of spreader. Consult your owner's manual for exact settings. Apply 50 percent more seed if you are attempting to sow a new lawn in the spring.

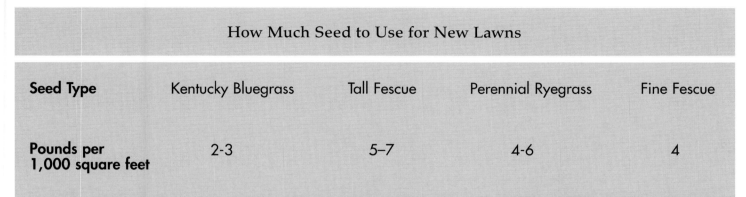

Above The general rule for seed application is to set your spreader to deliver between 5 and 10 seeds per square inch on the first pass, shown, and the same on the second pass. Rates of seed application vary, depending on the season, the type of grass seed, germination rates, and other conditions. When conditions are not favorable for seed germination, set your spreader to a higher setting. The photo shows the rule-of-thumb target of 15 to 20 seeds per square inch. *Inset* Rake the seeded surface lightly to mix seed with the top ⅛ inch of soil.

In the absence of specific recommendations from the seed packager, the rule of thumb for seed coverage is 15 to 20 seeds per square inch. Make trial passes with your spreader and adjust it until you achieve seven or eight seeds per square inch. Then spread seed in two passes, first in one direction and then in a perpendicular direction, to ensure even coverage of about 15 seeds per square inch. Bulk up seed with vermiculite or sand if your spreader delivers too much seed even when set on the lowest setting. Follow up with a light raking to work the seed into the top ⅛ inch of soil; a light rolling with an empty roller will ensure good seed contact with the soil.

Seeding sloped areas is difficult because the seed tends to run to low points when it rains. One solution is to contract with a landscaper who has hydroseeding equipment. Hydroseeding involves spraying a suspension of fertilizer, mulch, and water on to the prepared surface. Apply frequent light waterings to hydroseeded surfaces to keep them from drying out.

Stolonizing and Sprigging

There are two ways to plant sprigs by hand. You can broadcast, or stolonize, sprigs over prepared soil at a rate of 5 to 10 bushels per 1,000 square feet, cover with ¼ to ½ inch of soil, and then press the sprigs into the soil by rolling. Or, you can plant the sprigs (sprigging) in shallow furrows, 1 to 2 inches deep and 6 to 12 inches apart, depending on the grass variety and the sprig producer's spacing recommendations. Plant sprigs in furrows, end-to-end at 4- to 6-inch intervals, and cover with soil. Be sure a portion of each sprig remains exposed to light—ideally one-quarter of its length. Then lightly roll or tamp the planted area to press the sprigs into the soil.

Plugging

Plant plugs every 6 to 12 inches in furrows 6 to 12 inches apart. Or plant them in holes spaced 6 to 12 inches apart in each direction. If you're digging individual holes, using a bulb planter will make the job go quicker. Plant slower-spreading grasses, such as zoysiagrass, 6 inches apart because of their slow growth rate. Grasses that spread more quickly, such as St. Augustinegrass or Bermudagrass, may be planted farther apart. You can purchase plugs or make your own from

Plant plugs 6 to 12 inches apart.

unwanted areas of turf. Use a golf-green cup cutter to cut circular plugs, or use a sharp knife, such as a machete, to cut 2-inch-square plugs.

Caring for Your New Lawn

Consider these guidelines in caring for your newly planted lawn.

❑ *Traffic:* Minimize play and foot traffic on newly planted lawns, including sodded lawns, for at least three weeks.

❑ *Watering:* Plan for watering needs before you plant your lawn, not afterward. Insufficient water is the leading cause of new-lawn failure, and overwatering is not far behind.

For newly seeded lawns, set sprinklers to mist the surface four times a day, beginning at 7:00 A.M. and finishing at 6:00 P.M. The seedbed should be kept moist, but not saturated, to a depth of 1 to 2 inches. As seedlings grow to a height of 2 inches, reduce the frequency but increase the depth of waterings.

For plugs, sprigs, or sod, water at least twice a day, including once during midday. Keep the soil

Plant sprigs so that the top one-quarter of each plant is exposed. Space sprigs 6 to 12 inches apart, depending on the grass type.

Spreading a straw mulch over a new lawn gives it a better chance of survival by slowing evaporation, providing some shade, and dispersing drops of rainwater that might otherwise dislodge young seedlings.

moist to a depth of 1 to 2 inches. Check, however, to be sure that the soil does not stay saturated for long periods; otherwise the plants may not root. Reduce watering frequency to every second or third day once a plugged, sprigged, or sodded lawn has begun new root growth (about two weeks). After four weeks, a sodded lawn can survive longer periods without water.

❑ *Mowing:* Begin mowing newly seeded, sprigged, and plugged lawns after the grass has grown to a height of 3 or 4 inches. Cutting is best done with a reel-type mower because reel-types are less likely to uproot seedlings and plants, unlike today's mulching mowers, which have powerful vacuum action. If you don't have a reel mower, use a rotary mower with the throttle set low. For your first mowing, remove just enough (½ to ¾ inch) to give your lawn an even appearance. Next time, cut to the maximum height recommended for your type of grass, but do not remove more than 30 percent of the blade in any single mowing.

Do not mow a sodded lawn for at least 10 days after installation and not until the grass has begun to grow vigorously. Once again, if you use a rotary mower, set the throttle low to avoid lifting and chopping up pieces of sod. Once sprigs and plugs are established, regular mowing will encourage lateral spreading.

❑ *Mulches:* If the weather is dry or warm, spread a layer of straw mulch over seeded areas. Choose a clean mulching straw that's free of seed, such as wheat straw. Evenly spread about 50 to 80 pounds (one or two bales) per 1,000 square feet. In windy areas, stretch string over the mulch every few feet to keep it from blowing away. Avoid putting down a heavy layer that would inhibit grass growth. Burlap or agricultural fleece (a textile mulch that admits water and sunlight) are other mulches that will protect the seed from drying sun and wind. They are particularly helpful in preventing erosion and seed runoff when staked over seeded slopes. You may remove mulches approximately three weeks after germination.

❑ *Fertilizing:* Do not fertilize new lawns for at least six weeks. Then a light fertilization of ½ pound of nitrogen per 1,000 square feet is recommended. Afterward, fertilize according to the recommendations given for established lawns in the next chapter.

Newly sprouted grass plants thrive under the protection of a thin mulching straw.

chapter 8

Reducing Lawn Maintenance

The amount of time and money you spend maintaining your lawn depends a lot on your idea of what a lawn should be—not necessarily on what your lawn actually needs. Early lawns—those of the Middle Ages—did not require much maintenance. That's because they were inspired by glades or grassy openings in the forest, not by golf courses or pictures in magazines. These meadowlike lawns, made up of grasses and flowers, were planted among fruit trees, vines, flowers, and herbs and enclosed by fences or courtyards. There was no mowing. Grass was kept from growing too tall by trampling it into a soft, woven, matlike surface. If you can adjust your concept of a lawn to include taller grass, a mix of other plants in your turf, such as clover, and midsummer periods when your grass temporarily turns brown, you can achieve a low-maintenance lawn—and one that's closer to the original spirit of the lawn.

The Right Height

There are several reasons not to cut your grass too short. First, grass grows from the crown, not the blade tips. This trait makes grass ideal for lawns because it keeps on growing despite the regular mowing off of its upper stem, leaf sheath, and blades. This is also why it's important not to damage grass crowns by accidental scalping with the mower. No crown, no grass! Second, keeping grass on the longer side allows it greater surface area to carry out photosynthesis. This in turn results in healthier plants. Third, taller grass grows slower than shorter grass. You can use this simple fact to eliminate up to 20 percent of the mowing you do annually. That's a saving of about eight hours a year for the average lawn owner, not to mention the savings of gasoline and wear on equipment. Lastly, by keeping your grass at the upper end of its recommended mowing height, you can prevent most weeds from germinating—and thereby eliminate the need for herbicides.

When to Mow

Most cool-season grasses should be cut when they reach heights of 3 to 3½ inches, typically once a week as recommended in the table below. Cut warm-season grasses when they reach 2 to 2½ inches. Cut no more than one-third of the grass height at each mowing to avoid damaging the plants. If the lawn grows too high for you to cut off one-third the height and have an acceptable length, cut off one-third now and mow one-third off again in two or three days. Cutting more than one-third the height results in clumps of clippings that tend to lie on top of the lawn, decompose more slowly, and give the grass a less attractive, open, bristly appearance. In addition, short cutting will stunt or slow root growth and weaken the grass plants.

Recommended Mowing Heights	
Grass Type	**Inches**
Annual ryegrass	2–2½
Bahiagrass	2–3; final cut 1½
Bermudagrass	1–1½
Centipedegrass	1½–2
Fine fescue	2–2½
Kentucky bluegrass	2½–3
Perennial ryegrass	2–2½
St. Augustinegrass	2–3
Tall fescue	2½–3½
Zoysiagrass	1–2

Inset left A level lawn is more attractive and easier to mow than a lawn with depressions and bumps. *Inset* By setting cutting heights higher than most homeowners do, you can greatly reduce weed growth as well as mowing frequency. *Left* A lawn with a higher blade length is typically healthier and better able to resist disease.

What to Do with Your Lawn Clippings

Today's advice, contrary to what was recommended in the past, is to leave clippings on the lawn. The old belief that clippings contribute to thatch buildup has been proved false. Thatch is a buildup of old roots and stems, not grass blades. Leaving clippings where they fall not only saves you the labor of collecting and composting them; it also reduces the need to add fertilizer because the clippings themselves add nitrogen to the soil as they decompose. Clippings also act as a light mulch that helps to conserve soil moisture. However, there are exceptions to this advice. If you have neglected your mowing or must mow in wet conditions, the long clippings are likely to form heavy soggy clumps that cover the grass. In such cases, remove the clippings so that they do not smother the grass plants beneath them.

The idea of leaving clippings on the lawn is not new, but today's new mulching mowers, also

You can easily see the difference between grass that was cut with dull (left) and sharp blades.

SHARPENING A MOWER BLADE

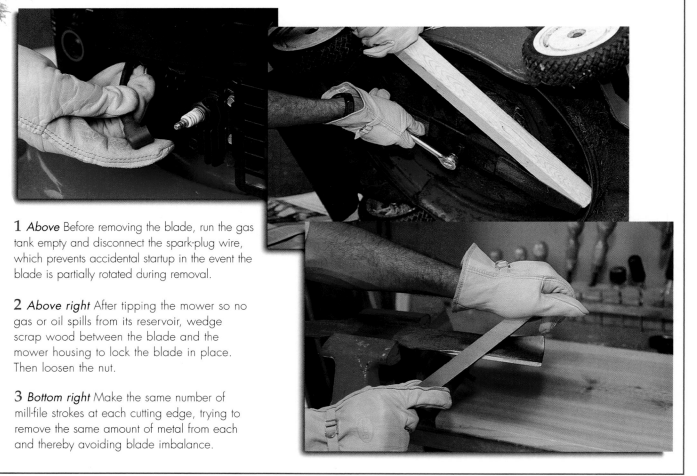

1 *Above* Before removing the blade, run the gas tank empty and disconnect the spark-plug wire, which prevents accidental startup in the event the blade is partially rotated during removal.

2 *Above right* After tipping the mower so no gas or oil spills from its reservoir, wedge scrap wood between the blade and the mower housing to lock the blade in place. Then loosen the nut.

3 *Bottom right* Make the same number of mill-file strokes at each cutting edge, trying to remove the same amount of metal from each and thereby avoiding blade imbalance.

called recycling mowers, make it even easier to leave clippings where they fall. The deck and blade designs allow these mowers to cut each grass blade several times, producing a finely chopped clipping.

Watering Frequency and Amount

Try to give your lawn the water it needs—and no more. This moderate approach conserves an important resource, saves money, and helps prevent grass diseases caused by too much water. How much water your lawn needs depends on the health of your lawn and soil, the amount of rainfall your lawn gets, and the climate. You may need as few as two waterings a year or as many as two a week.

The best approach to watering grass (and most other plants) is to follow nature's pattern of rainy periods followed by brief dry spells. Apply enough water all at once to penetrate to the roots, let the soil almost dry out, and apply water again. Grass signals that it needs water by losing its spring: When you walk across the lawn and see your footprints, your lawn probably needs to be watered.

To determine how much water your lawn needs, you need to consider several factors: the depth of your grass roots, your soil type and its "penetrability," your irrigation method, and of course, the weather. First, check to see how deep the roots of your grass grow. Add an inch to the average root

depth to arrive at a target watering depth. It makes no sense to waste water by watering to a level substantially deeper than your lawn's root zone.

Root depth depends on how much time you have taken to improve your soil and on the type of grass you are growing. Some grasses, such as tall fescues, have roots that reach 1 foot deep. Others grow to only half that, in even the best conditions. As your grass develops deeper roots, adjust your watering-depth target so that you continue to encourage roots to go deeper.

Check grass root depth by using a sharp spade or knife to cut several core samples from your lawn. Measure and average the root depths; then replace the samples.

Watering Dos and Don'ts

❑ Morning is the best time to water. Set out your sprinklers the evening before if you don't have an in-ground system. Otherwise, it's sloppy work to set up on grass that's wet with dew.

❑ Avoid watering under windy or hot conditions.

❑ Water deeply every 7 to 10 days during dry seasons. Don't worry if surface soil is dry, as long as the soil is moist a few inches down.

RULES OF MOWING

❑ Cut no more than one-third the height of the grass.
❑ Never scalp the lawn or cut below plant crowns.
❑ Mow only when the grass is dry.
❑ Mow with a sharp blade. Resharpen after every 10 hours of use. Bring the blade to a professional sharpening service once a year. Replace the blade as necessary.
❑ Change mowing patterns frequently to prevent compaction.

❑ Leave clippings on the lawn unless they are very long or wet.
❑ Rinse clippings off your mower after it has cooled to reduce the chance of spreading lawn disease.
❑ Cut grass at the high end of the recommended height range during hot weather.
❑ Cut at the low end of the recommended height range during cool weather or in shade.
❑ Make your last cut of the season at the low end.

❏ Do not water your lawn during rainy periods.

❏ Do not water in the evening unless you have no other option. Doing so helps to create the damp conditions that give diseases a foothold.

❏ In the South, do not water if nighttime temperatures drop significantly; the cold water can shock the grass plants and stunt their growth.

Ways to Reduce Watering

If you find that your lawn dries out quickly and needs more frequent watering than other lawns in your neighborhood, there are ways to minimize waterings. Keeping your grass relatively tall will help the plants reduce moisture evaporation by shading the soil. If you choose native grasses or those well adapted to your area when seeding, they will need less watering. Bluegrass is a guzzler; buffalograss is not. See Chapter 5, page 50, for more on grass types.

Improving your soil can also help reduce your watering needs. Try topdressing your soil with organic mate-

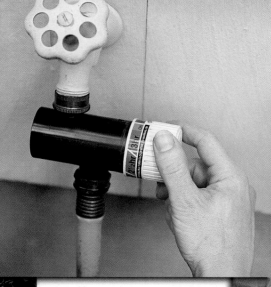

rial. Then work it into the soil using an aerator (with a core cultivator). Organic matter helps your soil hold water longer. In addition, aeration promotes deeper root growth. When combined with infrequent, deep waterings, aeration enables grass plants to take moisture from a greater soil area.

Keep chemicals off your lawn. Organic lawns require less watering than chemically treated lawns. Also, use a sharp mower blade to make cleaner cuts. (See photos on page 92.) Cleanly cut lawns look greener and cause less evaporation from the cut grass blades than raggedly cut lawns. Do not overfertilize.

One approach is to let nature decide the watering rate. Here you allow your lawn to brown out temporarily, or go dormant, when drought conditions persist. Usually this will not hurt a healthy established lawn, because the roots continue to live and are ready to send forth new shoots when conditions improve. There may be times during the year when it's just not worth trying to keep your lawn green. (Continue to water lawns less than a year old through dry spells.)

If you water your lawn manually, invest in a timer (either built into the sprinkler or installed at the outdoor faucet). With a timer, you can't

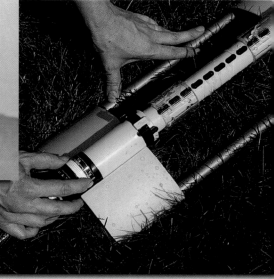

Sprinklers and timers can help manage watering chores. Shown here are a mechanical timer (above), a battery-powered programmable timer (left), and a sprinkler with a built-in timer.

forget to turn off the sprinkler. *Caution:* The flip side to using timers, the programmable ones, is if you're not careful you'll find that they turn on the system rain or shine. There's nothing more wasteful than sprinklers watering on schedule during a heavy rain storm. In-ground systems with soil or weather sensors avoid that problem. If you install an in-ground automated sprinkler system yourself, take care that it doesn't water your lawn more often than the grass needs.

Use a rain gauge to monitor rainfall. Don't water if nature has done the job for you.

Right To check water penetration, take a sample with a sharp spade or knife. Moist soil feels damp and will usually have a darker color than dry soil.

Place several cans around the area you plan to water. Run your sprinkler for 15 minutes and check the height of the water in the cans. Calculate the average height and use that figure to help you determine how long to water your lawn in the future.

Next, determine how much water is needed to moisten soil to the root zone. A good rule of thumb for most grasses is 1 to 2 inches per week. If you have porous soil that drains quickly, you would apply 1 inch of water twice a week. Conversely, if your soil holds water well, a good guess would be 1½ to 2 inches once a week.

To determine how long you should run your sprinkler to deliver the desired amount of water, wait for a four- to five-day dry spell. Then set out some empty cans in various locations on the lawn. Run your sprinkler or in-ground sprinkler system until the cans contain 1 inch of water. Then, wait 24 hours to allow the water to penetrate the soil (12 hours if your soil is porous—porous soil drains faster); then check the depth of the moisture penetration, as shown at left.

If 1 inch of water moistens soil to a depth well beyond the root depth, try the procedure again after your soil has dried, but turn off the sprinkler sooner. Conversely, if the root depth is not reached, try delivering more water. Keep accurate records of how long you need to run your sprinkler or sprinkler system to deliver the required amounts of water for your lawn, and then base future waterings on what you have learned from your observations.

If it rains during the week, decrease your watering by the amount of rain that fell. If it's hot and sunny or windy, you may need to increase the watering amount and frequency.

SPRAY-HEAD PATTERNS

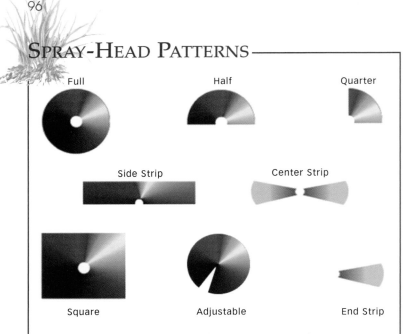

Full   Half   Quarter

Side Strip   Center Strip

Square   Adjustable   End Strip

Spray heads, the devices that deliver water to your lawn, are available in numerous designs to function in every conceivable landscape situation, from narrow and oddly shaped turf areas to large expanses of open lawn. The spray pattern of a head refers to the pattern of water distribution to the lawn. The broad selection of heads allows you to choose a pattern to fit even oddly shaped areas without overspray onto sidewalks, driveways, or other planting areas.

Pop-up spray heads are prominent only when the system is actively watering. When the system is off, reduced water pressure lets the heads sink down unobtrusively into underground sleeves.

In-Ground Lawn Sprinkler Systems

In-ground lawn sprinkler systems offer convenience at a price. First, there is the cost of the equipment and installation. Second, there is the time you must spend maintaining and repairing the system. If you live in a cold-winter climate, you must winterize your system every fall by draining all the water from it before the first freeze. Or you can hire professionals to drain your system by blowing compressed air through it. Most homeowners who take a low-maintenance approach to their lawns, especially those who reduce their lawn size and who are willing to tolerate some browning during adverse summer conditions, do not need in-ground systems.

However, if you plan on maintaining a sizable lawn and want to keep it green during the growing season, a permanent in-ground irrigation system can conserve water and save time, too. A properly installed system can deliver just the right amount of water when and where your lawn needs it, and it eliminates the need to drag portable sprinklers and hoses all over the yard. In-ground sprinkler systems also make sense for a vacation home that you visit irregularly or if you travel frequently and are not always home in summer to attend to your lawn's water needs.

How Permanent Sprinkler Systems Work

A typical in-ground sprinkler system delivers water via a network of underground pipes to all areas of a lawn. It consists of multiple control valves, each of which can either stop or start the flow of water to an area of lawn, or zone. Each zone consists of several sprinkler heads attached to buried pipes by risers (short vertical pipes) that are arranged to provide uniform water coverage to the grass in that area. Systems are divided into zones because household water pressure is capable of supplying only a limited number of sprinklers at one time.

(Continued on page 98.)

If you decide to install an in-ground irrigation system your-self, you won't need to be completely on your own. The major manufacturers offer free assistance to homeowners who want to design and install their own systems. One option is to have the manufacturer design your system and then install it yourself. Some manufacturers provide this design service free of charge and provide installation instructions and a shopping list of all the parts you'll need. Many companies also offer free advice over the phone. However, the easiest alternative is to hire a contractor to do the installation for you. Irrigation contractors own the right tools, know local codes and regulations, and can sometimes complete the whole job in an afternoon after an initial site evaluation.

If you choose to tackle the installation yourself, check with local building officials. Codes may require specific backflow or anti-siphon devices, which prevent irrigation-system water from mixing with your potable house water. You should also get okays from local utilities before dig-ging to ensure that you don't cut into their lines.

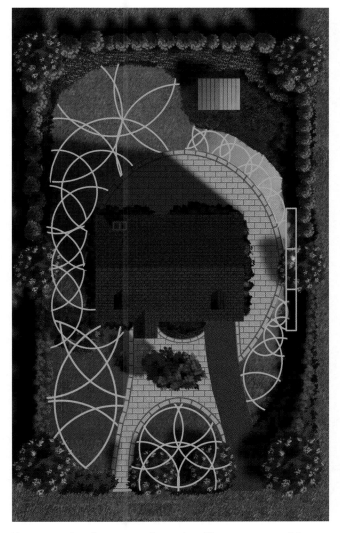

The arcs in this illustration indicate the different patterns of the spray heads used to make an efficient, full-coverage system.

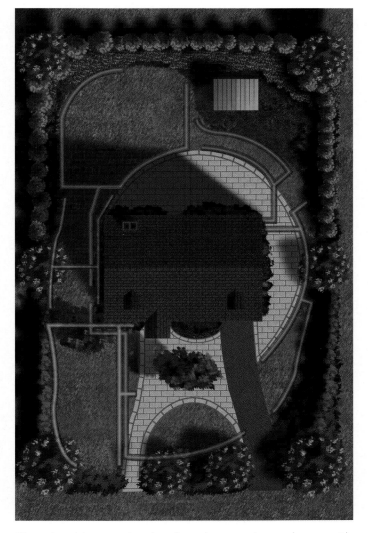

The colored lines on the plan show the system's pipe layout, with the various zones represented by different colors.

Strategically placed pop-up heads in this in-ground system water only the areas they are supposed to, without waste.

There are two types of in-ground sprinkler systems: manual and automatic. A fully automated in-ground system will typically include a programmable controller that allows you to schedule when and where various portions of your lawn will be watered. A signal from the controller activates a small servo-motor that opens or closes each control valve at the programmed time. Some automatic systems are equipped with moisture sensors (weather or soil) that override the controller program and prevent the system from turning on during rainy weather or after rain, while the soil remains moist. A manual system requires that you turn the control valves on and off by hand.

There are several types of lawn sprinkler heads, including sprayers that deliver a fine, mistlike spray and rotary heads that throw water in a wide circle, much like a portable rotary sprinkler does. Spray-type heads are specified for systems when accuracy of coverage is critical. Rotary heads deliver water to larger areas, so fewer are required. Pop-up varieties of each type of sprinkler head, spray and rotary, rise several inches above grade level when water pressure is introduced. This ensures that ground covers and low shrubs don't interfere with water delivery.

Sprinkler heads are installed in either triangular or square grid layouts. Make sure that the spray from one sprinkler head reaches the next one, for head-to-head coverage. For example, if you install sprinkler heads with a 12-foot radius, place sprinklers no more than 12 feet apart. Many sprinkler heads can be adjusted to control the amount of water delivered. They can also be adjusted to deliver water in a variety of patterns. A full head delivers water in a full circular pattern. The other circular patterns are half, quarter, and adjustable. Adjustable heads can water any part of a circle, from 0 to about 330 degrees. There are also rectangular and square patterns for

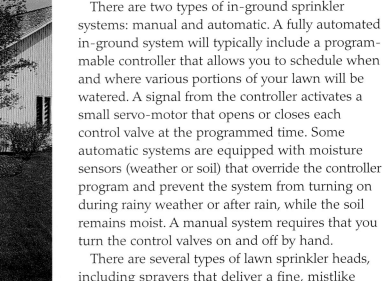

Controllers and timers for irrigation systems can be installed indoors or out. They can be mounted on interior walls, like this one on a garage wall (left), or on exterior walls inside waterproof panels. In warm-winter climates, controllers and timers are sometimes installed directly in the ground or on free-standing units.

A valve that controls an in-ground sprinkler zone is installed in a shallow trench for easy access and then covered with a panel to keep it out of sight.

also blast the petals off flowers. The plan shown on page 97 is designed for maximum turf irrigation efficiency, but it could be altered to water the planting beds as well. If you suspect uneven coverage—several parts of your lawn tend to be dry and brown, for example—try a simple test to be sure your sprinkler system is to blame. Place a half-dozen containers, such as tuna cans, throughout the affected area and run your system. Note the depth of water collected in each can and calculate an average depth. Perform the same test in areas that seem to receive adequate water (preferably at the same time of day to avoid variations due to fluctuations in water pressure), and make your comparison. If one area is receiving ¾ inch of water in an hour and another is getting only ¼ inch, make adjustments. Otherwise you will have to choose between two evils: continuing to deliver inadequate water to some areas and risking brown patches, or using more water than necessary elsewhere to ensure adequate coverage to areas with an inadequate rate of delivery.

narrow rectangles of turf or perfectly square areas, and there are end, center, and side-strip patterns for grassy pathways, side yards, and other tight spaces. (See the variety of spray pattern options available on pages 96–97.)

Assessing Your System

A well-designed sprinkler system will deliver water evenly to all grass areas. It's important to select heads that provide the right spray pattern for your needs but that also avoid overspray onto streets, paths, driveways, patios, buildings, and unwary passersby. Also, avoid placing a sprinkler where it will spray directly onto the trunks of trees and thereby damage the bark. The sheer force of the water pressure can score the bark, and constant wetting weakens it, making it more susceptible to pests and diseases. Misdirected spray can

This badly placed sprinkler blasts petals off these otherwise happy impatiens, illustrating the wisdom of planning the placement of all planting beds, trees, and lawn areas before you install underground lines. It's possible to change your mind and relocate a sprinkler head or two using flexible pipes, but it's better to avoid the inconvenience.

Turf Fertilization

Grasses require at least 16 different essential elements in their diets, most of which are available from the plants' surrounding environment. But the extraordinary growth demands of today's lawn owners usually mean that homeowners must help Mother Nature along.

Even if you are committed to having a low-maintenance lawn, you will need to fertilize it with nitrogen (N) to sustain thick, vigorous turf. In addition to bringing on deep green color, nitrogen is responsible for the sturdy growth and shoot density needed to fight off weeds and to stand up to disease, bugs, and traffic.

All these positive effects can easily turn into negatives if you use too much fertilizer or apply it at the wrong time. The common practice of fertilizing in early spring is actually not the best time in northern climes. It not only encourages excess blade growth, which means more mowing, but it also gives your weeds a boost and increases thatch! Excessive spring growth also produces thin-walled grass blade cells that are more prone to injury and disease. Late summer to early fall is the preferred time for feeding northern lawns; midspring in the South.

In addition to needing nitrogen, your lawn may need phosphorus (P) and potassium (K). Depending on where you live, your soil may naturally contain adequate levels of these elements. Aiding in root growth and improving establishment rates, phosphorus is needed in small amounts and tends to remain in the soil. Potassium plays an important role in enhancing your grass's resistance to cold, disease, drought, and wear, and is more prone to leaching from the soil. A soil test will help you determine which nutrients your soil needs. (See "Getting a Soil Test" pages 43–45.)

A fertilizer with the designation "complete" contains all big-three nutritional elements. The percentage of the bag's contents made up respectively of nitrogen, phosphorus, and potassium

Slow-Release Versus Fast-Release Fertilizers

	Advantages	Disadvantages
Slow-Release	Nitrogen released gradually Less apt to leach Low incidence of burning Fewer applications used Lasts longer	Higher initial cost Dependent on warm weather for release Takes longer for turf-grass response
Fast-Release	Immediate nitrogen availability Generally costs less Better known release rate Releases even in cold weather	More apt to leach, especially on sandy soils More apt to burn foliage May raise salinity of soil More frequent applications required May acidify soil and make it less hospitable to beneficial microorganisms May thin cell walls and make plants vulnerable to disease Requires more frequent watering

can be found by looking at the fertilizer grade. These three prominent numbers also tell you the percentage of nitrogen to phosphorus to potassium. For example, in a 50-pound bag of 20-10-10 grade, the ratio is 2:1:1, which means that 20 percent of the 50 pounds, or 10 pounds of the bag, is actual nitrogen; 10 percent (5 pounds) is phosphorus; and 10 percent (5 pounds) is potassium. The remaining 30 pounds of material in the bag may consist of additional elements such as iron and sulfur, as well as inert "filler" ingredients. Fillers are used to help ensure even distribution of the product and are frequently made from organic materials such as finely ground corn cobs.

Ratios are helpful in choosing which fertilizer to use for specific purposes. Those with a 1:2:2 ratio, such as a 6-12-12 fertilizer, are lower in nitrogen but higher in the nutrients desired when planting new grass or renovating old lawns. Fertilizers with high-nitrogen ratios of 2:1:1, 4:1:2, or 3:1:2 are frequently used for maintenance applications. They contain N, P, and K quantities closer to the plant's ongoing needs and are available in grades of 12-6-6, 16-8-8, 20-10-10, 12-4-8, and so on.

In considering which bag of fertilizer is most appropriate for your yard, be sure to read the back label for the guaranteed analysis of the contents. If your soil test indicates that you don't need to add phosphorus or potassium, choose a bag with

Fertilizer ratios and grades tell consumers how many pounds of nutrients are contained in 100 pounds of the product. Fertilizer ratios indicate the relative amounts of nitrogen (N), phosphorus (P), and potassium (K).

a low numeral or zero for that element. For example, a bag of 20-0-5 would have no phosphorus.

In addition to checking the grade, you should also determine what type of nitrogen has been used, water-soluble or water-insoluble. Water-soluble nitrogen, once watered into the soil, can be immediately used by grass plants. Ammonium nitrate, ammonium sulfate, and urea are examples of this quick-release form of nitrogen. These provide a rapid green-up, but they also have drawbacks, as shown in the table "Slow-Release Versus

NITROGEN FERTILIZERS

As discussed in the text, the fertilizers listed below are commonly available at nurseries and garden centers.

Fast-Release Nitrogen Fertilizers
Ammonium nitrate
Calcium nitrate
Ammonium phosphate
Ammonium sulfate
Urea

Slow-Release Nitrogen Fertilizers
Sulfur-coated urea
IBDU (isobutylidene diurea)
Ureaformaldehyde
Bone meal
Methylene urea
Activated sludge
Dried poultry waste
Soybean meal
Composted manure
Alfalfa meal

Fast-Release Fertilizers" on page 100. Water-insoluble nitrogen, found in slow-release fertilizers, must first be broken down by soil microbes into forms grass plants can use. These slow-release sources include synthetic organics, like ureaforms, or those derived from natural organic materials, such as composted manures.

To spread the release of nitrogen over time, fertilizer companies can also manipulate the size of particles and sometimes coat them as well. Because these forms take longer to dissolve, they release nitrogen at varying rates. Common examples are isobutylidene diurea (IBDU) and sulfur-coated ureas.

When buying fertilizer, opt for the water-insoluble types or other slow-release forms. Using slow-release fertilizers will allow you to reduce the amount of time you spend behind your spreader. They last much longer and don't have to be applied as frequently as quick-release fertilizers, saving you money as well as time. Determine the type of fertilizer you have by reading the guaranteed analysis on the bag. *Note:* Many fertilizers have a combination of both fast-release and slow-release types of nitrogen. You should check carefully to find products that derive a majority of their nitrogen from slow-release sources.

The optimal time to apply fertilizers is when the grass roots and blades are actively growing. In the North this growth season occurs during the early to mid fall, when weed competition is minimal and fertilizing produces healthy root growth. This timing also allows plants to build up needed carbohydrate stores with just a moderate amount of topgrowth. For northern lawns, you should divide the annual amount of fertilizer and apply two-thirds in early fall and the remainder in mid to late spring, after the lawn's initial green-up. Because the grasses in southern lawns have a larger blade size and grow more vigorously, they will need at least two applications of fertilizer each year. Do the first about three weeks after the initial spring green-up; then fertilize again in late summer. You can add supplemental quick-release nitrogen between these times if weak growth and poor color indicate that it's needed.

For low-maintenance lawns, you should be applying 2 pounds of nitrogen per 1,000 square feet per year in the North and 2 to 4 pounds in the South. This may require an adjustment, given your specific growing environment, soil test results, the lawn's condition, and the type of fertilizer you use, whether slow- or fast-release. You can consult your

TIPS ON USING LAWN FERTILIZERS

- ❑ Test soil to determine grade and amount of fertilizer to use.
- ❑ Apply no more than 1 pound fast-release nitrogen per 1,000 square feet in a single application.
- ❑ Cool-season lawns should receive most of their yearly fertilizer in the early fall.
- ❑ Fertilize warm-season lawns from early spring until late summer.
- ❑ Use slow-release nitrogen whenever possible, especially on sandy soils.
- ❑ Wait until warm-season grass becomes dormant before fertilizing areas overseeded for winter color.
- ❑ Use only the amount called for, based on your lawn's square footage.

- ❑ For quicker application and to avoid a striped fertilizer pattern in the grass, use a rotary spreader, which applies fertilizer more evenly.
- ❑ Spread the fertilizer in two directions for each application.
- ❑ Apply fertilizer to dry grass, and water well immediately afterward.
- ❑ Sweep up any fertilizer spilled on paved areas and save for later use.
- ❑ Don't use leftover lawn fertilizer on trees, shrubs, annuals, or perennials.
  Too much nitrogen on these plants stimulates stem and leaf growth and decreases flower and fruit production.

In the fertilizer industry, the term *organic* is used to refer to any product containing carbon in its chemical structure. This means that man-made forms such as urea-formaldehyde are called organic along with "natural" fertilizers, such as composted manure. While both kinds of materials supply slow-release nitrogen to your grass, natural, or nonsynthetic, fertilizers do more than just add nutrients to the soil. They improve the overall condition of the soil and increase the number of beneficial microorganisms residing in it. Unfortunately, natural fertilizers would need to be spread in large quantities to meet lawn fertilization requirements. So, the best strategy is to use natural fertilizers to supplement a yearly dose of synthetic fertilizer.

Cooperative Extension Service for local recommendations. Quick-release fertilizers are usually applied at a rate of 1 pound of nitrogen per 1,000 square feet. Slow-release fertilizers usually require a higher rate of application to deliver their nitrogen. Follow the manufacturer's instructions and check the calibration of your spreader, as well as the square footage of your lawn, to ensure that you are applying the right amount. Remember, more is not necessarily better with fertilizers. Applying too much may "burn" your lawn and promote thatch formation and disease.

Keep in mind that lawns kept under irrigation throughout the summer or located in areas receiving heavy rainfall will require more nitrogen than their unwatered counterparts. Sandy soils are more prone to leach nutrients, but using water-insoluble fertilizers will help nutrients remain in the soil longer. Leaving grass clippings on the lawn over the course of a year will add about 1 pound of nitrogen per 1,000 square feet, so you can figure accordingly. The total amount of nitrogen that you'll need per year also varies with the type of grass you are growing. For example, Kentucky bluegrass and perennial ryegrasses require more fertilizer than the fescues, while in the South, Bermudagrass, zoysiagrass, and St. Augustinegrass need more than bahiagrass, centipedegrass, or carpetgrass.

Thatch Control

The best way to control thatch is to avoid a buildup in the first place. Here are some maintenance practices that will help: Cut grass at the recommended height for your turf at regular intervals to avoid depositing too many clippings at one time. Fertilize only in the fall to reduce excessive growth. Promote microbial life by maintaining a proper soil pH. Aerate your lawn once a year.

If thatch does begin to accumulate to undesirable levels, apply a topdressing of a compost-and-soil mixture prior to aerating in the spring and fall. The organic matter will promote microbe activity, which in turn will help decompose thatch.

Nuts on the thatching rake allow you to adjust the angle of the sharp tines (shown) to control depth of penetration.

chapter 9

Controlling Weeds

NOT LONG AGO, white clover was considered a fashionable lawn plant. Pleasant to look at, it increased the nitrogen content of soils and helped to break up compaction. But since it didn't look like grass, it was classified as a weed. Today, as homeowners reconsider their definition of lawn weeds, clover is slowly regaining its status as a desirable lawn plant. If you were to look through a comprehensive list of weeds, you might be amazed at the plants you'd find there. But a weed is really best defined as a plant growing where you don't want it. That can include tall fescue growing amid Kentucky bluegrass and the drought-proof flowers of yarrow spreading beyond the flower border.

Because weeds are survivors, designed to make a go of conditions that don't favor most other plants, they will always be with us, looking for a chance to establish themselves. Rather than cast a disparaging eye on anything growing in the lawn other than your chosen lawn grass, you are better off accepting that diversity is a fact of nature. Your task is to decide which weeds you can tolerate and which must go, whether because they are too noticeable, overly aggressive, or a health hazard, like poison ivy.

Even an attractive, unaggressive plant like yarrow might be considered a weed growing in a lawn.

A Healthy Lawn: Your Best Ally

Some gardeners consider weed control a type of battle to be won. Another approach is to regard weeds as a warning that all is not well with your lawn and to take steps to improve conditions. Keeping your lawn growing vigorously by providing an optimal growing environment will help minimize weeds and prevent other problems. When weeds do creep in, you need to identify the conditions or practices encouraging their growth.

Identifying Weed Species

To make informed decisions, you will first need to correctly identify the various plants growing in your turf. Weeds are either narrow-leaved and grasslike or broad-leaved; the majority of weeds are broad-leaved. They also have varying life cycles that are important to know for you to effectively time your control measures.

Annual weeds are the most common, living for one growing season and reproducing only from seed. Cool-season annual weeds germinate in late fall or winter; they then flower, produce seeds, and die in the spring. They can be especially troublesome in dormant southern lawns, and that is why some people overseed with cool-season grass for the winter. Warm-season annuals go through their complete life cycle from the spring to the fall of the same year. These weeds are most problematic in northern grasses that go dormant in the heat of summer. The important point to remember about all annuals is, because they reproduce only by seed, they can be controlled by disrupting their growth any time before they set seed.

Left Addressing the problems that cause weeds can help save your lawn from a weed takeover like this. *Insets left* Poison ivy leaves emerge reddish and glossy, turning dull green as they mature. *Inset* White clover is enjoying renewed acceptance as a lawn plant, but its presence may indicate a problem in the soil.

Ground ivy, also called gill-over-the-ground, spreads by aboveground stolons, as shown, and by underground rhizomes.

Perennial weeds are the long-lived ones. They don't die after flowering, and many reproduce both by seed and by vegetative means such as rooting rhizomes. Some perennial weeds, like dandelions, have fleshy taproots that can produce a new plant from just a piece of root left in the ground. Creeping weeds, such as ground ivy, spread from underground rhizomes and above-ground stolons. Perennials are more difficult to get rid of, but they are as vulnerable during their seedling stage as the annuals.

Cultural Measures Count

Mowing to the right height, as discussed in Chapter 8, is one key to preventing weeds. In addition to promoting healthier grass, keeping your turf on the long side helps block sunlight from weed seeds just waiting to germinate. When weed seeds are evident, catch your grass clippings and dispose of them, rather than redistributing them on the lawn.

Maintaining optimal fertility is also paramount, as a dense lawn makes it difficult for weeds to compete. Critical, too, is the timing of fertilizer applications. Applying fertilizer in the summer to dormant northern grasses is a sure-fire way to energize any weeds present. On southern lawns, applying fertilizer in the fall encourages cool-season weed growth. As explained in Chapter 8, fertilize northern lawns

in the fall and southern lawns in mid spring. That will ensure strong growth as the grasses enter their main growing seasons. Another way to make life inhospitable for certain weeds is to rectify compaction and poor drainage. Lastly, thwart the growth of shallow-rooted weeds by watering deeply but infrequently, and allow the top ½ inch of soil to dry out between irrigations.

Weeds are opportunistic plants, and sometimes ridding your lawn of them entails changing those conditions conducive to their growth. Areas compacted from frequent foot traffic, and therefore prone to growing plantain and crabgrass, might be better served by the installation of a walkway or steppingstones. If weeds congregate in hard-to-mow areas under or adjacent to fences and walls, consider eliminating them by using edging and mulches. If a bare area should develop, don't leave it open to weed invasion; reseed as soon as possible.

Unmaintained borders are often breeding grounds for weeds, which eventually find their way into your lawn.

The Nitty-Gritty of Weed Removal

Although prevention through appropriate cultural methods is your first line of defense against weeds, there comes a time when you need to roll up your sleeves and get after them. On small areas, the old-fashioned approach is still the best—pull them out by hand. Make weeding a regular part of your maintenance routine, completed in the cool of the day, when the soil is damp. Hand weeding may take a bit longer than using selective herbicides, but it's a lot better than worrying about the kids and pets getting into the toxic compounds you must otherwise use and then safely store. Besides, if you add up the time it takes to drive to the nursery to buy the herbicides, to wash down the applicator, to study the directions and mix the proper solution, to apply the proper solution and, as often as not, to bring expired herbicides to facilities for proper disposal, you will find that the no-herbicide approach doesn't take much more time, if any.

Weeds with shallow, fibrous roots, such as chickweed, yield well to pulling. Grip them as close to the soil as possible, and then rock them back and forth to loosen them before giving a yank. Success in digging out weeds with taproots depends on getting the entire root. Ideally, these perennials should be removed as seedlings, when they are less firmly rooted. But in reality, we frequently don't notice them until the lawn turns yellow with blossoms. For larger, established plants, using a spade works well, but smaller ones can easily be taken care of with a long-handled prong-type weeder. This tool or a pointed trowel is also quite useful when popping out weeds that have a rosette of leaves right at ground level, such as plantains and other compact weeds.

Removing Deep-Rooted Weeds
STEP One
Use a garden spade to remove deep-rooted weeds, such as dandelions. Push the spade 6 inches into the turf, about two finger widths from the weed's stem. Do not undercut the weed, or you may leave a large enough piece of root to grow back.

STEP Two
Rock the spade or tool to slightly loosen the section of turf and underlying soil. Grab the weed at the stem and work it loose from the turf. You don't need to shake soil free from the roots before discarding weeds in a compost bin.

Removing Shallow-Rooted Weeds

Shallow-rooted weeds, such as plantain, can be removed using a weeding tool. Boiling water can spot-kill weeds that appear in walks and driveways, but be careful or its overflow may kill nearby desirable plants.

Using Flame

Organic farmers have successfully used fire to kill weeds. "Flaming" is done with a gas torch that emits a narrow flame. The object is to heat the plant's sap until its cell walls burst. Just the clear cone of gas surrounding the flame is actually passed across the foliage until it starts to soften and wilt.

Because the roots aren't injured, you will need to repeat this treatment on perennials when the foliage regrows. Eventually the weed will use up its carbohydrate stores and be unable to reproduce or put out new growth.

Shallow-rooted weeds can be loosened with a weeding tool or spot-killed with boiling water.

A spade or trowel can reach deep roots of the dandelion.

Using Plants to Fight Plants

Scientists are researching improved ways to control weeds. One method involves using fungi to attack targeted plants. Called mycoherbicides, these fungi and other naturally occurring compounds show promise for inhibiting weeds. Research is also focused on allelopathic grasses, such as perennial ryegrasses and tall fescues, which have properties that cause them to make soils inhospitable to certain weeds. As new cultivars come out, look for those that can be overseeded into your lawn to offer a measure of protection against certain weeds.

Herbicides

When looking at large areas of lawn contaminated by weeds, most people consider resorting to herbicides. In fact, it is difficult to go to a local garden-supply store without seeing shelves of products all promising to quickly rid your lawn of weed problems. Unfortunately, herbicides toxic to your weeds are often hazardous to your health, and to the health of other living things that come into contact with them. Certain components of herbicides, such as the chemicals 2,4-D and arsenic, may pose serious health hazards and are under scrutiny. Many herbicides do not break down quickly but remain active in the soil, increasing both health and contamination risks.

What is a beleaguered homeowner to do? If you cannot avoid using herbicides, look for the least toxic products and spot-treat affected areas only. Avoid products containing the most controversial chemicals, such as 2,4-D.

Using an herbicide to spot-treat hard-to-weed areas is sometimes called for.

Look also for formulations that break down rapidly in sunlight and by microbial action; such products do not leave residual chemicals. Unfortunately, many of the rapidly biodegradable solutions now available are nonselective. This means that any foliage that comes in contact with them, including your turf grasses, will be injured or killed off. These products are appropriate only for spot-treating weeds in the lawn or for use along fence lines, walls, and other structures.

SOME LEAST-TOXIC HERBICIDES

Herbicidal Soap (Superfast by Safer) is made from potassium salts of fatty acids derived from naturally occurring plant oils and animal fats. Contact with herbicidal soap damages plant cell walls, causing dehydration and tissue death. Soaps are broad-spectrum and nonselective and work best on seedlings. Deep-rooted weeds and perennials will require repeated applications. Soaps break down completely within 48 hours and carry an EPA rating of IV. CAUTION. There is also an herbicidal soap for use specifically on lawn moss.

Glyphosate (Roundup, Kleen-up) is a water-soluble salt that inhibits a plant's ability to produce certain essential amino acids, thus hindering new growth. This is a non-selective, broad-spectrum herbicide with an EPA rating of IV. CAUTION. Glyphosate is biodegradable and not harmful to life in the soil, where it has an average half-life of less than 45 days. Effects may not be seen for 7 to 10 days.

Glufosinate-Ammonium (Finale by AgrEvo), a metabolic compound originally derived from a soil bacterium, this herbicide interferes with photosynthesis, killing annual weeds and even many perennial weeds in one to four days. While nonselective and broad-spectrum, it affects only those plants that have been treated. It is biodegradable with an average half-life in soil of 7 to 20 days. It carries an EPA rating of III. CAUTION.

Weed-A-Way, by Safer, is an example of a selective broad-leaved weed herbicide that does not contain 2,4-D. Made from synthetic chemicals MCPA, MCPP, and dicamba, it carries an EPA rating of IV. CAUTION.

The Environmental Protection Agency (EPA) tests and rates the toxicity of all herbicides, requiring that one of four "signal" words be used as warnings on labels. They are, from most to least toxic: I. DANGER; II. WARNING; III. CAUTION; IV. CAUTION. *Signal words for the same formulation may vary with the degree of concentration.* Use any herbicide, no matter how mild, with great care and never when it's windy; always follow label directions strictly. Look for herbicides made of naturally occurring products, such as fatty acids, that are quickly decomposed by soil microorganisms.

Common Lawn Weeds

Here are the most common weeds and recommended means of dealing with them.

Annual bluegrass

Annual bluegrass (*Poa annua*) Frequently found in compacted infertile soils, this light green, low-growing grassy annual prefers cool-season growth but can be found all year. Sudden lawn brown-out with the heat of summer or prolific weed seed production in spring signals its presence. When seed appears, rake the grass upright. Then mow and bag clippings.

Crabgrass (*Digitaria* species) Few summer lawns are without this warm-season annual that branches out its low-growing wide leaves. There are two varieties: The more upright type is called large, or hairy, crabgrass; the more prostrate type is called smooth, or small, crabgrass. The

Crabgrass

latter has purplish stems. Both types produce prolific seed heads that stand out like long fingers. Mowing high, removing seed heads, and maintaining dense turf are essential to its control.

Purslane (*Portulaca oleracea*) Forming reddish mats of succulent oblong leaves and stems, this warm-season annual likes hot, dry weather. Its fibrous root system allows for fairly easy pulling, but don't leave any stem fragments behind, because they are capable of developing new roots. The plant bears small yellow flowers followed by urn-shaped capsules that release tiny black seeds.

Purslane

Prostrate spurge (*Euphorbia prostrate*) Prominent in summer, this warm-season annual grows in rosettes of green hairy-leaved stems. A related variety, spotted spurge (*E. maculata*), is similar but has a purple leaf spot. Generally low-growing with a taproot, prostrate spurge exudes a milky sap from broken stems.

Prostrate spurge

Chickweed

Perennial chickweed

Ground ivy in flower

Top Dandelion flower
Above Seed head
Left Taproot

Common plantain

Annual chickweeds (*Stellaria* species) Delicate in appearance, these low-growing annuals may remain green all year in mild climates. Preferring shade and areas of thin grass, annual chickweeds can be distinguished from their perennial cousin by their small, heart-shaped, bright green leaves and petite white flowers that resemble stars. Pulling, raking to bring them upright, and mowing all help to deter them.

Perennial chickweed (*Cerastium vulgatum*) Also called mouse ear for the shape of its hairy dark green leaves, this perennial forms dense mats of low growth. It spreads by seeds and creeping rootstocks and prefers infertile soil. Digging up, raking upright, and mowing help keep this perennial in check.

Ground ivy (*Glechoma hederacea*) This plant is also called gill-over-the-ground. Because of its vigorous growth, this one-time ground cover is now considered a hard-to-control weed. A cool-season perennial, ground ivy has rounded leaves with scalloped edges growing along square stems. It thrives in moist shade but spreads readily in the sun as well. Harbingers of later seed, lavender to blue funnel-shaped flowers appear in early spring. At the first sign of growth, pull or hoe up plants. Rake upright in spring and mow close.

Dandelion (*Taraxacum officinale*) The bright yellow flowers of this cool-season perennial soon turn to delicate spheres of seeds. Dandelions bloom from spring to frost, with new seedlings appearing in the fall. It's best to dig out the fleshy taproot when the plant is in flower and consequently low on the carbohydrate reserves needed for regrowth.

Common plantain (*Plantago major*) Rosettes of waxy green leaves appear, especially in dry compacted lawns. This cool-season perennial spreads both by new shoots and seed formed on seedheads resembling rat tails. Low mowing and poor fertility encourage growth.

Research at Iowa State University has shown that corn gluten meal, a byproduct of milling corn, has herbicidal effects. Additionally, corn gluten contains 10 percent nitrogen and serves as a slow-release fertilizer. Field testing on Kentucky bluegrass has shown that common weed populations, such as crabgrass, clover, and dandelion, can be reduced by more than 80 percent with successive treatments over several years. The most susceptible weed species are purslane, black nightshade, common lambsquarters, creeping bentgrass, curly dock, and redroot pigweed. Corn gluten is strictly a preemergent herbicide that works by inhibiting root formation, and so timing of application is critical. Ideally, it should be applied three to five weeks before the target weeds germinate. If applied once weeds have established roots, it will only boost their growth.

Reports on the effectiveness of this product when used on broad-leaved and grassy weeds have shown uneven results. A number of variables come into play, such as amount of rainfall, breakdown rate by microorganisms, and timing of application. But initial research and field reports look promising for corn gluten's future use as an herbicide. Corn gluten meal is sold by the bag or ton and is available under a number of names, among them WEEDZSTOP, Concern, and W.O.W.

Buckhorn plantain (*Plantago lanceolata*) Also a cool-season perennial, this plantain has slender long leaves with three to five prominent veins. Arising from a rosette of leaves with a taproot, the seed heads look like short cylinders atop long spikes. To discourage this plantain, you should alleviate compaction, improve fertility, and raise mowing height.

Nimblewill (*Muhlenbergia schreberi*) Showing up in late spring, this warm-season grassy perennial becomes obvious when it turns straw-colored in early fall. Its leaves branch off fine wiry stems that contrast with surrounding grasses. Spread by stolons and a shallow, fibrous root system, it prefers hot, dry conditions and either forms circular patches or appears throughout a lawn.

Buckhorn plantain

Nimblewill

chapter 10

Fighting Lawn Diseases

WHETHER YOUR LAWN SERVES as an impromptu soccer field or as the main element of your landscape, its appearance and vigor are important. Keeping it healthy is more a matter of sticking to basic management practices than of looking to chemical solutions. The importance of paying attention to mowing height, aeration, drainage, irrigation, and fertilization really can't be stressed enough. Coupling these practices with the use of suitable grass cultivars and healthy soil will give your lawn an advantage over the harmful microorganisms normally found in most yards.

The Plant Disease Triangle: Pathogen, Host, and Environment

Fortunately, it takes more than the presence of pathogens (disease-causing microorganisms) to bring on infection in lawns. You also need a host—that is, a grass susceptible to a particular pathogen—and environmental conditions that foster disease. Conditions favoring pathogens vary by pathogen but generally include warm weather and extended periods of moisture, from rain, humidity, irrigation, or poor drainage. Other conditions, such as drought and high heat, encourage problems because they reduce the grass's ability to fight off infection. These three elements—pathogen, host, and environment—make up the "Plant Disease Triangle." Any one factor on its own cannot initiate disease. Problems begin when all three come together.

Fungi: Friends and Foes

Dwelling in your soil and upon your lawn are myriad threadlike forms of plant life called fungi. Some of them, such as *Trichoderma harzianum*, are important components of healthy soil. They may facilitate nutrient uptake by grasses and keep disease-causing fungi in check through competition for resources. Problems arise when the disease-causing group becomes dominant. The initiators of most lawn diseases, these fungi are spread by wind, rain, grass clippings, and even your lawn mower. They can overwinter and remain dormant in soil or thatch for long periods of time, awaiting just the right conditions before growing. Like a person, your lawn becomes a target for infection if stressed. Although you cannot keep pathogens off your grass, you can sidestep disease by manipulating the other two factors—host and environment.

To keep your lawn from becoming a host, choose the right grass for a given location and keep it healthy. Given the range of disease-resistant grasses available today, you have a good chance of avoiding certain diseases right from the start. (See Chapter 5, "Choosing the Right Grass," page 50, for more information on disease-resistant grasses.)

You might not be able to change the weather, but you can lessen its negative impact on your grass. Well-aerated lawns with good drainage and air circulation will experience fewer moisture problems. In areas prone to brown patch, some homeowners remove the morning dew (which contains nutrient sugars that contribute to brown patch formation) by lightly hosing down the lawn or pulling a hose across it. Good cultural practices do make a difference in the health of a lawn.

Left Pythium blight can destroy a grass stand in a day. *Inset far left* Despite its name, pink snow mold appears pinkish only under certain conditions and doesn't limit itself to snow-covered turf. *Inset left* Named after woodland fairies whose nighttime dancing was said to wear down the grass, fairy rings are difficult to remove but may disappear on their own.

Ironically, often the very actions we take to improve our lawns aid in the establishment of diseases. For example, frequent, light waterings encourage shallow root growth, making the grass vulnerable to drought stress. Watering late in the day leaves a wet grass canopy that is conducive to fungal growth. Also, excessive use of high-nitrogen fertilizer promotes unnecessarily lush top growth that is more prone to disease. And using a dull mower blade shreds grass tips, providing a potential entry point for infection.

Is It Really Disease?

Before mowing is the best time to assess your turf's state of health. While you are out picking up fallen twigs or removing other items from the lawn, stop to take a careful look at any areas that appear wilted or off-color or that otherwise stand out from their surroundings. If you do note changes, don't rush to blame them on disease; there are numerous other possibilities. For instance, a general browning-out of a cool-season grass during high summer is likely just summer dormancy, the grass's protective response to drought and heat. Dull, wilted, bluish gray turf is the grass's signal that it needs

water. General yellowing and stunted growth may be attributable to a lack of iron or nitrogen. Ragged leaf tips and a whitish cast usually indicate that your mower blades need sharpening.

Consider also the kinds of activities that have recently occurred in your yard. Perhaps the bright green rings surrounding dead grass are courtesy of the neighbor's dog, and the brown patches near the garage could be the result of a gasoline spill. While problems, these eyesores are limited in scope and can usually be rectified with fertilization, irrigation, or spot reseeding. If your turf's decline cannot be explained by such causes, look more closely.

Keep Your Eyes Open

Many diseases will leave you with bleached-out dead turf. If your lawn has reached this point, then you have not only lost the grass but also the opportunity to determine what caused the problem. Diseases are progressive in nature, especially during hot, humid weather. So it is important to observe your lawn regularly if you want to spot disease symptoms that are apparent only early on. Look for spots or banding, color changes, or signs of decay on grass blades. When you examine affected turf, ask yourself some questions. What

The grass in the "bull's-eye" above was killed by repeated sprays of dog urine; excess nitrogen from the urine forced the surrounding grass out of dormancy in early spring, producing the circular tuft of lush, deep green grass.

The guilty party below seems to realize that she's been asked to pose next to incriminating evidence.

is its shape, size, and color? Does it feel slimy or dry? If there are patches, how are they distributed across the lawn? Give the grass a tug to check for rot. Lastly, venture out early in the morning while the lawn is damp with dew to look for signs of fungal mycelia. These fine, cobweb-like threads disappear with the day's heat and sun. Identifying lawn diseases can be difficult. Damage may not be apparent until turf is stressed by drought and heat. If your lawn's symptoms stump you, you can take a sample to a reputable nursery, a Cooperative Extension Service lab or your state university plant pathology department. Before taking samples, be sure to call and obtain specific sampling instructions.

When disease does get a foothold in your lawn, you need to take immediate steps to contain it. Start by bagging your lawn clippings and not adding them to your compost pile. Next, avoid walking through infected turf, especially when it is wet. Now is the time to review your management practices to determine why your grass became susceptible. Then decide which actions are needed to

Patches of pink snow mold, called Fusarium patch when the disease strikes a lawn without snow cover, may start off orange-brown and turn light gray before turning a salmon color.

improve your lawn's growth environment and to alleviate the conditions that foster fungal growth. Keep in mind that as weather conditions change, they may no longer promote fungal growth, thereby allowing the problem to resolve itself naturally. But if disease symptoms continue, you may decide that you need to apply a fungicide.

TOPDRESSING WITH COMPOST

Research has shown that microorganisms present in well-aged at least one-year-old organic compost can suppress turf grass diseases. Scientists at Cornell University note that effective control of dollar spot, brown patch, and gray snow mold can be achieved with monthly applications of such "suppressive" compost. Additionally, regular topdressing also lessens the severity of pythium blight and necrotic ring spot infections.

Although the theory is still under investigation, plant pathologists believe that the presence of "antagonistic" microorganisms in these aged organic materials are what help them to suppress disease. Usually fungi, they are called antagonistic because they have an adverse impact on disease-causing microorganisms. They kill them, damage them, or out-compete them for food and habitat resources.

Recommended suppressive topdressings include composted manures, pulverized tree bark, leaf compost, composted garden debris, sludge (such as Milorganite), or agricultural wastes. Amending mature organic composts with commercial "innoculants" that contain beneficial microorganisms yields even greater disease suppression. Current researchers are working to identify which microorganisms fight which pathogens in hopes of creating products formulated to ward off specific diseases. In the meantime, topdressing with a ¼-inch layer of well-aged compost once in early spring and again in fall may not only help to decrease your thatch layer, it might also give your lawn the added nutrients and microorganisms it needs to keep disease at bay. See Chapter 3, page 28, for more information about using compost.

A Word About Fungicides

Fungicides have been the traditional means of treating lawn diseases. While fungicides do clear up certain problems, they unfortunately may make turf vulnerable to new ones. This happens primarily because fungicides kill off the beneficial, disease-suppressing microorganisms and fungi as well as targeted organisms. If your disease symptoms continue unabated and you feel the need to use a fungicide, use it sparingly and follow the package directions. Of the mineral-based fungicides, elemental sulfur is considered the least toxic to humans and is available in a wide range of products.

A Look at the Future

Nonprofit organizations, such as the Bio-Integral Resource Center (BIRC) in Berkeley, Calif., are studying nontraditional ways of preventing and resolving lawn diseases. These include using neem oil (which contains sulfur compounds), biological fungicides, and fungicidal soaps. Scientists are also investigating the potential for disease-prevention roles of fungi and other microorganisms. Another avenue of research involves the positive correlation between soil nutrients, such as calcium, and a grass's resistance to disease. There is much to learn, but we do know that keeping the complex ecosystem of your lawn in balance is key.

Identifying Diseases

Grass cultivars named below are just a sampling of available grasses with resistance to various diseases.

Spring Through Fall (Cool, Moist Conditions)

Fairy rings Caused by more than 50 varieties of fungus, the rings vary in size and appearance but all form in soil high in woody organic matter, usually from buried debris or tree stumps.
❏ *Look for:* Rings of fast-growing, dark green grass with centers of weeds, thin turf, or dead grass. Midsummer and fall rings are more apt to be composed of dead grass.

Fairy rings of dark green grass are often large and may be accompanied by mushrooms, especially if conditions are moist.

LONG-TERM PRACTICES THAT HELP PREVENT DISEASE

❏ Choose recommended grass seed mixtures. Then if lawn disease does develop, not all grass types will be affected.
❏ Look for improved or disease-resistant cultivars when renovating or starting new lawns.
❏ Water your lawn only early in the day, from sunrise until 11 A.M.
❏ Water only when needed, and then to a depth of 6 to 8 inches.

❏ Maintain adequate lawn aeration and drainage.
❏ Never cut off more than one-third of the grass length at one time.
❏ Keep mower blades sharp.
❏ Keep thatch to ½ inch in height.
❏ Apply appropriate fertilizer, and correct nutrient deficiencies, especially calcium.
❏ Prune and thin trees and tall shrubs to increase air circulation and sunlight exposure.

❑ *Management:* The rings are difficult to remove unless completely dug out to a minimum depth of 1 foot. Aerating the ring area to improve water penetration and fertilizing to minimize color variation are helpful.

Stripe smut Causes yellowed, stunted growth in 6- to 12-inch patches.

❑ *Look for:* Development of characteristic black stripes of erupted spores along grass blades that later become dry, shredded, and curled.

Stripe smut results in poor growth and long, yellow-green grass blade streaks that turn black.

❑ *Management:* Use resistant cultivars like the bluegrasses 'Adelphi' or 'Midnight'. Maintain adequate fertilization. Water well, mow frequently, and bag clippings.

Necrotic ring spot Although the fungus is active during cool, moist periods, the damage frequently doesn't show until later, when turf is stressed.

❑ *Look for:* Circular "frog-eye" patterns of 6 to 12 inches with matted, straw-colored grass surrounding a tuft of green grass. As infection advances, roots and crowns may turn brown to black. Thatch may decompose in affected areas, giving them a sunken, or "donut," appearance.

❑ *Management:* Overseed with disease-resistant cultivars of tall fescue and perennial ryegrasses, or use bluegrasses such as 'Classic', 'Eclipse', or 'Columbia'. In Canada, choose the bluegrasses 'Barblue', 'Nassau', 'Princeton', and 'Adelphi'. Water to lessen drought and heat stress. Avoid excessive fertilizer use. Remove excess thatch and maintain aeration and drainage.

Drechslera melting-out and leaf spot formerly Helminthosporium Exhibiting two phases, this disease is especially destructive on overfertilized, lush bluegrasses. Cloudy, moist weather in the 70° to 85°F range brings on the telltale leaf-spot phase.

❑ *Look for:* Distinctive dark purple spots that develop into buff-colored oval lesions with a dark brown or purple margin. Blades progress to yellow and then turn tan. During the melting-out phase, rot develops in roots and crowns.

❑ *Management:* Use resistant bluegrass cultivars such as 'Eclipse', 'Nuglade', 'Midnight', 'Alpine', 'S-R 2000', or 'Princeton 104'. Avoid excessive nitrogen fertilizer, water infrequently but deeply, mow high, aerate, and remove excess thatch.

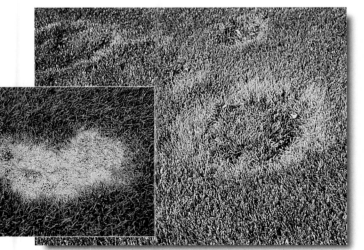

During spring and fall, high-maintenance lawns planted with bluegrass or red fescue are prone to necrotic ring spot.

Drechslera leaf spot is a two-phase disease fostered by evening watering and excessive use of nitrogen fertilizer.

Also known as Rhizoctonia blight, brown patch is most active when grass remains wet and temperatures reach 80° to 90°F.

Summer

Brown patch Prevalent during moist, hot weather on overfertilized lawns.

❑ *Look for:* Dark, water-soaked-looking grass turning to browned-out, circular areas, several inches to several feet in diameter. Frequently some green leaves persist within the patch, and roots remain intact. Blades may have irregular ash gray lesions with a dark brown margin running along one side. On short turf, a 2-inch unsightly "smoke ring" of gray mycelium may encircle the patch in early morning.

❑ *Management:* Use improved cultivars, such as ryegrasses 'Repell III' and 'Prelude III', 'Scaldis' fine fescue, or 'America' bluegrass, and use a slow-release nitrogen fertilizer. Water deeply but infrequently, mow high, remove excess thatch, and improve aeration and drainage.

Dollar spot Affects low-nitrogen lawns, especially when stressed by drought and when heavy dews are prevalent.

❑ *Look for:* Mottled, straw-colored 4- to 6-inch patches on lawns with taller grass. Grass blades

Named after the initial silver-dollar-size spots that appear on closely mowed lawns, dollar spot often signals a turf that is nutritionally deficient.

have light tan bands with reddish brown margins spanning across them. Patches may merge to form large, irregular areas. Grayish white cobwebby mycelium may be present in early morning.

❑ *Management:* Overseed with a blend of improved cultivars such as the bluegrass 'Adelphi', perennial ryegrass 'Manhattan III', and fine fescue 'Reliant'. Maintain adequate nitrogen and potassium fertility, water deeply when necessary, and remove excess thatch. If your grass is prone to dollar spot, remove morning dew by dragging a hose across the lawn.

Rust Appears on low-fertility, compacted, or shady lawns when growth slows during hot, dry weather.

❑ *Look for:* Initial small yellow flecks that develop into pustules releasing yellow, orange, red, or dark brown spores. From a distance the turf appears orange or yellow, and colored spore residue rubs off if touched.

❑ *Management:* Use rust-resistant cultivars of ryegrasses such as 'Palmer III' and 'Repell III' and new cultivars of Kentucky bluegrass such as 'Challenger' and 'Eclipse'. Provide appropriate fertilization and irrigation; prune low-hanging tree branches to reduce shade; maintain aeration; and mow frequently, bagging clippings.

Rust is aptly named for the color your grass turns when this self-limiting disease is present.

Pythium blight A serious, rapidly spreading disease involving the entire grass plant, Pythium blight occurs on poorly drained soils that have a wet grass canopy. Look for it when nighttime temperatures plus relative humidity equals 150.

❑ *Look for:* Sudden appearance of 1- to 6-inch reddish brown, wilted patches, which turn to streaks as they enlarge along drainage patterns.

Grasses infected with Pythium, also known as "grease spot" or "cottony blight," frequently die.

In early morning, the grass is slimy, dark, and matted. White cottony mycelium may be present when the grass is wet. As it dries, the grass turns light tan and shrivels.

❑ *Management:* Improve drainage and air circulation, avoid overwatering, aerate, reduce excess thatch and avoid nitrogen fertilizer during warm weather. Check calcium levels and add lime if deficient. Observe closely for spread and consult your Cooperative Extension Service if the disease progresses.

Fall Through Spring (Cold, Moist Conditions)

Typhula blight (gray snow mold) Strictly a cold-weather disease, Typhula blight appears where snow cover has melted, especially in areas where snow has drifted or been piled.

❑ *Look for:* Irregular 2- to 24-inch patches of bleached-out, matted turf covered with moldy, grayish white mycelium. Tiny black or orange-brown spherical sclerotia (hard fungus bodies)

may be observed embedded in the leaves and crowns of infected plants.

❑ *Management:* Avoid heavy nitrogen fertilization in late fall to allow new growth time to harden off before winter. Keep thatch to a minimum and grass height lower as winter begins. Avoid piling snow onto your lawn, and prevent compaction on important turf areas by limiting activity on them when they're covered with snow. Rake in early spring to promote drying and reduce matting. Provide a light spring fertilization if damage is present.

Fusarium patch (pink snow mold) This disease develops from late fall to early spring during cool, moist, cloudy weather, with or without snow cover.

❑ *Look for:* Small, light tan to rusty brown circular patches that may grow to 2 feet and become ringlike as interior grass regrows. When the grass is moist, salmon-colored mycelium is visible in sunlight. There are no sclerotia present.

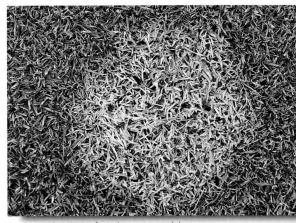

Scattered spots of pink snow mold contrast clearly with dormant turf.

❑ *Management:* Fertilize in late fall, once grass growth ceases, with a slow-release nitrogen fertilizer. Mow the lawn, keep thatch low, and don't allow leaves or debris to remain on the lawn over winter. Rake lawn well in early spring and follow with a light fertilization if damage is present.

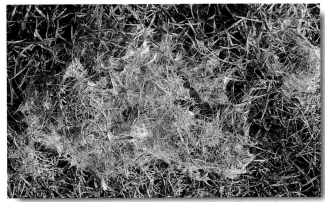

Gray snow molds are more apt to develop when early, wet snow falls on unfrozen ground.

chapter 11

Managing Lawn Pests

INSECT PROBLEMS, LIKE DISEASES, are apt to develop when conditions are favorable to them. As the weather warms up in spring, insect populations and activity increase. Your first and best line of defense against these pests is to provide optimal growing conditions for your lawn. The objective is to cultivate a thick, healthy turf that isn't overly attractive to pests as either habitat or food. Being more resilient, such lawns are also better able to survive the inevitable foraging of insects.

Preventive Tactics

There was a time when lawn insects could count on finding a great meal just about anywhere they went. Today their pickings are far slimmer, thanks to new grass cultivars containing endophytic fungi that repel or kill insects attempting to eat them. Incorporating such grasses into existing lawns or planting new lawns with them will markedly cut down on problems resulting from ground-level pests.

Insects are also especially fond of the lush new growth typically found on highly fertilized lawns. Avoiding over-fertilization and applying fertilizers at the right time will supply the necessary nutrients to your grass without fostering the fast, weak growth that is so attractive to pests. If and when the bugs do arrive, you can further thwart them by having encouraged beneficial insect predators to your yard.

IPM, An Eco-friendly Approach

For many years, insects in general have been viewed as invaders that should be attacked with various toxic chemicals. While such actions may take care of the immediate problem, they usually create a host of others. Today, an ecologically sound concept called Integrated Pest Management, or IPM, is receiving serious recognition and support among home gardeners, professional landscapers, and scientists alike. With IPM, the yard is viewed as an ecosystem with components that are interdependent and where every action has a wide-ranging impact. The goal of IPM is to keep insects, diseases, and weeds at tolerable levels using the least toxic methods available. Techniques include planting pest-resistant cultivars, following appropriate lawn-care practices, inspecting regularly for problems, encouraging beneficial insects, and—when necessary—spot-treating affected areas.

Let's face it, bugs are here to stay. Most of them are actually desirable and serve important functions in biological processes, such as decomposition. Others are considered beneficial because their diet includes the insects chomping on your grass. Studies have shown that predators, such as ants and ground beetles, are able to remove up to 74 percent of Japanese beetle eggs and up to 53 percent of fall armyworm pupae from pesticide-free plots within 48 hours. Before reaching for the insecticide, wait a while to give these natural enemies of pests a chance to bring your problem under control. Read on to learn more about the numerous insects that call your yard home, as well as how you can keep the upper hand.

Visible Clues to Insects

Knowing your local pests and their life cycles is the key to determining whether lawn damage is due to insects. The rest is a matter of keeping your eyes open. Most insects are large enough to be visible, so don't wait for your grass to start dying to find out there's a problem.

Left A lawn attacked by grubs will have patches of dead, dying, or wilted grass. But if injury is moderate, the lawn may recover. ***Above left*** Adult Japanese beetle ***Above right*** Japanese beetle larvae, or grubs, are considered the single most damaging lawn pest in the U.S.

EARTHWORMS ARE MORE THAN FISH BAIT

Earthworms are a sure sign of excellent soil conditions.

Abundant in moist, heavy soils, earthworms are a natural component of healthy lawns. Their diet of dirt, organic matter, and plant litter, is excreted in the form of a rich digestive byproduct called castings. These hardened small piles can be found scattered across the ground. While initially they can be felt underfoot, castings will eventually break down, providing your lawn with a dose of natural fertilizer. Worm castings are sold commercially for this very purpose.

In addition to helping provide nutrients for plants, earthworms aid in thatch decomposition. They also improve soil aeration and increase water penetration through their extensive burrowing.

Some evening, the presence of sod webworms may become apparent when you see their adult form, a buff-colored moth, zig-zagging across the lawn. And consider those June beetles banging against the screens at night or the Japanese beetles eating your roses—they should alert you to the fact that their larvae may be damaging your grass roots. Another clue to the presence of underground insects is small upturned areas where skunks dig by night and birds congregate by day.

Looking closely at the lawn, even using a magnifying glass, will enable you to see signs of chewing or the tiny light spots indicative of sucking insects. You might also note the tunnel openings of mole crickets or actually see thatch-level insects such as armyworms, chinch bugs, leafhoppers, and aphids.

The next section "Harmful Insects to Watch for" (see this page) describes some common lawn pests and the damage they cause.

Becoming an insect sleuth isn't difficult, and your persistence will pay off. The byword here is *vigilance*—making a regular habit of closely observing your turf. And remember, just a few bugs are nothing to worry about. You only need to take action when the population approaches damaging levels, remembering that extermination is not a reasonable goal.

Harmful Insects to Watch for

The following information is divided into two categories: insects causing damage aboveground and those that work underground.

Insects That Do Damage Aboveground

Chinch bug The premier pest on St. Augustinegrass lawns, chinch bugs are found on other grasses as well, in all but the coldest climates. Black, winged, and ⅕ inch long, they live in the thatch layer where eggs are laid at the root line. Most damaging are the tiny red nymphs, which thrive on sap sucked from grass stems.
❑ *Look for:* Yellow patches that don't improve with watering, starting in June, in hot, dry, sunny lawn areas. Look

Adult chinch bug and nymph

under the grass canopy to see nymphs and adults. An alternative is to use the Water Flotation Test. (See

"Testing for Insects" on page 126.) If you see 20 to 25 bugs over five minutes, you need to take action.

❏ *Management:* Maintain minimum fertilization, irrigate regularly, keep thatch low, and raise mowing height. Encourage beneficial big-eyed bugs, and use endophyte-enhanced, resistant grass cultivars. (For more on big-eyed bugs, see "Beneficial Insects," page 132.) For St. Augustinegrass, 'Floralawn' and 'Floratam' are resistant varieties; 'Floratine' is considered tolerant of chinch bugs. If cultivars don't cure the problem, consider spot treatment with insecticidal soap or pyrethrin.

Sod webworm Nighttime feeders that usually aren't noticed until damage is obvious, these small, green, spotted caterpillars feed on grass roots, crowns, and leaves. The adult form, a small, whitish gray to brown moth, can be seen in the evening taking short, jerky flights across the lawn.

❏ *Look for:* Irregular brown patches of short or uneven turf in early spring, especially in hot, dry areas. On close inspection, you may see silken grass tunnels used for daytime shelter and green waste pellets in the thatch. To check the population level, use a soap drench over affected areas; 15 webworms per square yard requires action.

Adult moth form of sod webworm

❏ *Management:* Damage can be outgrown with an extra dose of fertilizer in the spring and increased irrigation. Thatch should be minimized and ground beetles encouraged. *Bacillus thuringiensis* (BT) is effective on young larvae and *Steinernema* nematodes are a useful biological control. Endophyte-enhanced perennial ryegrasses, tall fescues, and fine fescues are recommended resistant turfs that will thwart hungry webworms.

WATCH WHAT YOU'RE STEPPING ON

It pays to know what insects look like throughout their life cycle, because they metamorphose, or change form, as they grow. Born with rigid or semi-rigid outer skins, insects would have a difficult time growing if they weren't able to shed this covering as they outgrew it. Some insects—such as beetles, lacewings, and moths—start life as grublike larvae and then evolve to an intermediate stage at which they are called pupae. Finally after more molting, they assume their adult form, which looks completely different from the earlier stages. Such a total transformation is called a complete metamorphosis.

Most people are familiar with the caterpillar-to-butterfly cycle, but many people are not aware what lady beetles and lacewings look like in infancy. During this larval stage, these and some other beneficial insects have an especially voracious appetite for pests. Unfortunately for these helpful bugs, they are so ugly as larvae and so unlike their familiar adult forms that unknowing gardeners often squash them.

Other insects do not experience the same degree of transformation; instead they go through a gradual metamorphosis. These insects are called nymphs in their immature stage, when they look like smaller versions of their adult forms; mantids are examples of such insects.

The photos below show the complete metamorphosis stages of lady beetles from egg to larva, pupa, and adult.

Fall armyworm At 1½ to 2 inches, these striped, brownish green nighttime feeders are twice as long as webworms. Basically a southern insect, they move north either as spring-migrating moths or as caterpillar armies seeking food in summer and fall.

❏ *Look for:* Chewed, bare, circular areas, similar to the damage of webworms, except that armyworms don't make tunnels. With large infestations, damage can accumulate quickly.

Fall armyworm

❏ *Management:* Use of *Bacillus thuringiensis* (BT) spray, some botanical insecticides (such as natural pyrethrum), and parasitic nematodes (such as *Steinernema carpocapsae*), will help. Encourage natural predators such as braconid wasps, ground beetles, and birds. (See page 129). Maintain optimal cultural conditions to encourage new growth.

Leafhopper These tiny, wedge-shaped, green, yellow, or brown flying bugs suck sap from leaves while injecting toxins into the grass. Lawn damage is usually slight.

❏ *Look for:* Mottled whitish patches with leaves browned along the edge and curled at the tips. When disturbed, leafhoppers will (what else?) hop away or, if adults, fly.

❏ *Management:* Maintain lawn vigor through regular cultural practices. Encourage lacewings, parasitic wasps, and ladybugs.

Leafhopper

Insecticidal soap or botanical insecticides, such as pyrethrins and rotenone, may be used for severe infestations.

Green aphid These tiny pear-shaped insects (sometimes called greenbugs) feed on the juices of grass blades while injecting a salivary toxin. They have been causing serious damage to Kentucky bluegrass lawns in some midwestern states since the mid-1970s.

Green aphid, or greenbug

❏ *Look for:* Yellowing of turf, frequently in sunny locations but sometimes extending out from the base of shade tree trunks. Close inspection will reveal the aphids.

❏ *Management:* A good old-fashioned hosing down will discourage aphids from returning. Natural predators such as lady beetles, lacewings, big-eyed bugs, ground beetles, and parasitic wasps should be encouraged. For large infestations, use insecticidal soap. Botanical insecticides, such as pyrethrins or neem, may be warranted.

Insects That Do Damage Underground

White grubs These root-eating larvae of the scarab beetle family include Japanese beetles, June bugs, rose chafers, and the black turf grass ataenius. Grub size and characteristics vary, but generally grubs are plump, whitish gray, and C-shaped with brown heads, and they have three pairs of legs. Watching in summer for adult Japanese beetles, which are metallic green with copper wings, or June bugs, which are reddish brown nocturnal fliers, will help with identification.

❏ *Look for:* Wilted, bluish gray grass that initially looks like drought damage in late spring and becomes dried and browned-out turf. With the roots eaten, the turf will roll back when pulled on. Once soil heats up to 60°F in spring, grubs may be observed in the top few inches of dirt. Unless the grass is already in poor condition, control is usually not necessary until you have 10 to 15 grubs per square foot.

If you've got beetles eating your shrubs (left), their larvae are probably eating your grass roots (above).

❏ *Management:* Before using milky spore disease to combat Japanese beetle grubs, check with your Cooperative Extension Service to see if the spore is effective in your area. Studies have indicated that milky spore, under certain conditions and especially in colder climates, is less efffective than previously thought.

Since these beetles prefer moist soil for laying eggs, one tactic is to water deeply but infrequently during the summer. White grubs are also susceptible to parasitic nematodes, such as *Steinernema carpocapsae*. Neem oil and pyrethrins can be used if indicated. If damage warrants reseeding, turning over the soil and either hand-picking the grubs or leaving them exposed for birds may serve as a short-term alternative.

Billbugs The C-shaped, small white larvae of this weevil causes more damage than the adult. Found more commonly in northern states, billbugs prefer Kentucky bluegrass, feeding on the stems, crowns, and eventually roots.

❏ *Look for:* Irregular dry patches the color of whitish straw that develop by midsummer. When affected grass is tugged, it breaks off at the root line, exposing hollowed-out stems packed with sawdust-

Billbug

like material. Unlike its condition after grub damage, the turf will not feel spongy. You may note some of the legless larvae underground.

❏ *Management:* Nematodes are showing promise for this difficult-to-control bug. Use of resistant bluegrass varieties, such as 'Park', 'Arista', 'NuDwarf' and 'Delta', or endophyte-enhanced ryegrass and fescues, is recommended. Rotenone may be used for spot treatment.

Mole crickets These large crickets with short, stout forelegs feed on grass roots and tunnel through underground root zones. They are especially damaging pests in the light, sandy soils of the southern and Gulf plains. They prefer bahiagrass but feed on whatever grass is available.

❏ *Look for:* Small tunnel openings and spongy ground along with browned, dry patches of turf. Use a soap drench as described in "Testing for Insects," next page, and observe for three minutes. Two to four crickets per 4 square feet are significant.

❏ *Management:* Follow good cultural practices to encourage deep root systems and to keep thatch low. Use low-nitrogen fertilizer to avoid developing overly succulent growth, and mow high. Research done at the University of Florida has shown promising results using a parasitic nematode, *Steinernema scaperisci*. Also, ground beetles are a beneficial predator.

Mole cricket (right) and mole cricket lawn damage

TESTING FOR INSECTS

In addition to the time-honored method of parting the grass and looking around, the following techniques will expose the damaging insects in your lawn.

Soap drench. Useful for flushing out sod webworms, armyworms, mole crickets, and caterpillars. Mix 5 to 6 tablespoons of dishwashing liquid in a 2-gallon sprinkling can full of water. Then drench 4 square feet of lawn with the solution. Observe the area for three minutes, counting the number of bugs that emerge.

Water float. Used for chinch bugs. Cut both ends off of a 2- to 3-pound coffee can and push it 2 or 3 inches into the soil at the margin of a yellowed area of grass. Fill the can with water and maintain its level above the grass surface for five minutes as you watch for chinch bugs to float to the top.

Sod lift. Used for grubs, billbugs, and rose chafer larvae. Using a spade, cut three sides of a 1-foot-square piece of sod about 2 inches deep, and lay back the sod flap. Check grass roots to see if they are chewed off, and sift through the top several inches of soil to count larvae. Replace sod and water well.

So You've Got Bugs

Having done your homework and identified the particular insects damaging your lawn, you now must decide what, if anything, to do about them. There are general guidelines for how many insects in a given area constitute a threat. The tricky part is that vigorous lawns can withstand greater numbers of pests than those under stress. Thus a healthy lawn might not show signs of injury in spring despite having a high number of Japanese beetle grubs per square foot. But the same lawn, when semi-dormant in late summer, might develop significant problems with just 6 to 10 grubs per square foot. Before making treatment decisions, consider how healthy your lawn is to start with, where the insect is in its life cycle, and how much damage you can tolerate.

If the population numbers and extent of grass injury warrant action, your first step might be to physically remove as many bugs as possible. (See "Mechanical Bug Removal," below.) Next, reduce thatch levels and compaction where they are problems. You should also consider whether your lawn needs some extra tender loving care to help it recover more quickly. Don't cut the grass too short or add water stress to its list of woes!

If despite your best efforts, pest populations aren't restrained through the more benign efforts of cultivation, grass selection, and competition from beneficial insects, you may need to use microbial controls, botanical insecticides, or insecticidal soaps. These have the environmental advantage of rapidly breaking down when exposed to sunlight, heat, and water; so they don't persist on vegetation or in the soil. They are generally considered less toxic to humans than synthetic products, but they can still upset the ecological balance in your yard and cause more harm than good if used improperly. Be sure to read labels and follow directions carefully, including the use of protective masks and clothing—some of these substances are severe irritants. When using sprays, avoid the middle of the day when they will be less effective, and time applications to take advantage of pest life cycles. Check with your local Cooperative Extension Service to learn about the specifics for your location and pests.

Mechanical Bug Removal

When pests are visible and large enough, removing them via the "pick and squash" method is an option for the non-squeamish. Try the following on insects you cannot see.

For chinch bugs: Prepare a soap drench with 2 tablespoons of dishwashing liquid and 2 gallons of water in a watering can. Thoroughly water an off-color patch of lawn and then cover it with a flannel sheet. Wait 15 minutes; then scrape clinging bugs off the sheet and into a garbage can, and close the cover.

For sod webworms: Drench the target areas with a soap solution and watch for the worms to climb up from the thatch layer. Rake them up and dispose of them in the garbage or in water.

Natural Controls

Several other natural controls are also effective on lawn pests. Consider using the biological controls, botanical (plant-derived) insecticides, or insecticidal soaps described below when mechanical controls are not feasible.

Biological insecticides The advantage of using either biological or microbial insecticides is that they are only harmful to specifically targeted pests. They are not injurious to wildlife, humans, or other soil microbes or insects. Furthermore, they don't leave toxic residues behind to worry about. They do come with an admonition, though. The mold spores, bacterial spores, and other living organisms that make up these products can produce allergic reactions in some people. Handle them with care, wear protective clothing, avoid inhaling them or rubbing them on your skin, and follow all provided directions.

❑ *Bacillus thuringiensis* (BT) is composed of a crystalline protein produced by the spores of a soil bacterium. When ingested by targeted pests, it destroys their gut lining, stopping their feeding and killing them. Insect-specific strains are sold as dusts, emulsions, and wettable powder. BT is highly selective and viable for only a few days after application. Apply in late afternoon for the best results.

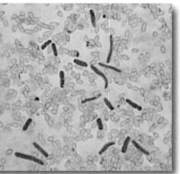
Bacillus thuringiensis, or BT

❑ *Bacillus popilliae,* or milky spore disease, has been the chief biological agent for Japanese beetle control. Its efficacy is now in question, however, especially in northern soils. Check with your Cooperative Extension Service for local recommendations. Only one or two applications of milky

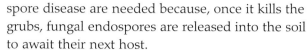
Bacillus popilliae, or milky spore disease, is a powder applied with a tablespoon at 4-foot intervals.

spore disease are needed because, once it kills the grubs, fungal endospores are released into the soil to await their next host. However, this product is not effective for other kinds of white grubs.

❑ *Steinernema glaseri* and *Steinernema carpocapsae* are predatory nematodes useful for attacking lawn pests such as billbugs, sod webworms, and white grubs.

Steinernema carpocapsae, a beneficial nematode

These microscopic, wormlike creatures live in moist soil and attack the larvae of certain pests. Beneficial nematodes are not harmful to plants, and different strains are sold to target specific pests. The use of predatory nematodes is a quickly growing area of horticultural research that shows much promise. For more on nematodes, see page 133.

Botanical insecticides Botanical insecticides are not targeted to specific pests, and they often kill beneficial insects as well. They are best used only as a last resort, when more directed methods fail. Although they do not persist long in the environment, botanical insecticides can be quite toxic when applied, so handle them with care and always follow package directions, including wearing protective clothing.

❑ *Pyrethrins* are made from extracts of pyrethrum flowers, two species of chrysanthemum. Known for their ability to "knock-down" flying insects, pyrethrins are frequently combined with synergists, such as piperonyl butoxide, which increases the pyrethrins' toxicity and length of residual action. Used against aphids, armyworms, beetles, caterpillars, leafhoppers, and other pests, pyrethrins are also toxic to fish and some beneficial insects.

❑ *Rotenone* One of the oldest botanical insecticides, Rotenone is extracted from the roots of Asian derris plants.

Caution: This slow-acting general insecticide is highly toxic to fish and moderately so for mammals. It is also very irritating to the respiratory tract.

❏ *Sabadilla,* one of the least toxic botanical insecticides, is made from the seeds of the Venezuelan plant sabadilla *(Schoenocaulon officinale).* Used as a dust or spray to kill grasshoppers, armyworms, webworms, aphids, and chinch bugs, this insecticide breaks down rapidly in sunlight. Sabadilla is highly irritating to the respiratory tract and eyes.

❏ *Neem* is derived from an oil extracted from the Indian neem tree. It is effective on multiple fronts—repelling insects, stopping them from feeding, inhibiting molting, and suppressing growth. Neem affects leaf-chewing beetles, caterpillars, and other insects going through metamorphosis. It has low toxicity for mammals.

Mycoinsecticides The *Beauveria bassiana* fungus was discovered in 1835, but it was not until recently that its potential as an insecticide was realized. Now this common soil-borne fungus has found a use

TAKING COVER

Using insecticides and herbicides derived from botanical, biological, or synthetic materials still requires basic precautions. Read product labels thoroughly and apply these products with great care. If your clothing becomes wet with the pesticide, remove it immediately. Shower directly after using these products and before changing into uncontaminated clothes. Following is a list of basic protective clothing and gear that you may need.

❏ Long-sleeved shirt, pants, and socks made of tightly woven material (all cotton). Do not leave skin exposed!

Heavy-duty rubber latex gloves, not just household gloves, protect hands from accidental chemical or toxic splashes or sprays, yet allow needed flexibility. Gloves that extend to the forearm and fit snugly around the wrist (like those shown above) provide the best protection.

❏ Waterproof, unlined gloves
❏ Waterproof footwear
❏ Hat, scarf, or hood to completely cover scalp and to overhang face
❏ Goggles
❏ Disposable dust mask designed for pesticide dusts
❏ Tight-fitting respirator when using liquid sprays. Respirators contain activated charcoal cartridges that filter pesticide vapors from the air. Make sure it's approved by the National Institute of Occupational Safety and Health (NIOSH).

Note: Be sure to rinse off your waterproof gear and pesticide applicator with plenty of clean water before removing your protective apparel. Avoid handling the outside of the contaminated clothing—use gloves if necessary—and, if it will not be laundered immediately, place the clothing in a sealable plastic bag. Wash these garments separately from your regular laundry. Pre-soak them in a pre-soaking product; then wash them on the highest temperature setting for a full cycle with detergent. If the clothing has any residual pesticide odor after the rinse cycle, repeat the washing procedure until the odor is gone. Air-dry the wet clothes on a line; then wash the washing machine by running it through the wash cycle with detergent but without clothes. Or simply throw the clothes away.

Those birds reveling in the backyard dust know what they're doing. Finely ground particles in such dust baths damage the exoskeletons of insects hitching a ride on the birds' backs. Diatomaceous earth, a dust used to control caterpillars, works on the same principle. Composed of fossilized remains of single-celled plants called diatoms, these ancient deposits are quarried and then processed to form a dust. People and animals are not bothered by this material; but on exposure, many soft-bodied insects are mortally wounded because it destroys either their protec-tive outer layer or gut. Used primarily for garden pests, it will also help con-trol aphids and ants in the lawn.

If you plan to use diatomaceous earth to control pests, be sure to buy the type meant for horticultural use. Diatomaceous earth sold for use in swimming pool filters is processed differently and is not effective for pest control.

Diatomaceous earth

in Integrated Pest Management (IPM) programs because of its low toxicity and ability to kill insect pests without harming most beneficials. Results vary, but generally this fungus offers good control of sod webworms, fall armyworms, billbugs, chinch bugs, aphids, and white grubs, among others.

A thorough spraying of targeted pests is necessary because successful infection is dependent on direct contact with the fungus. Under favorable conditions, the fungal spores penetrate the insect's body, where they secrete a killing toxin. Death of the host usually takes three to seven days.

Beauveria bassiana is now being produced com-mercially and has been registered with the EPA for use in landscapes.

Insecticidal soaps Insecticidal soaps are made from the potassium salts of fatty acids. On direct contact with susceptible insects, these acids disrupt the structure and permeability of their cell membranes, causing desiccation and death. Most effective on soft-bodied insects, including beneficials, these soaps have a minimal impact on ladybug larvae and parasitic wasps. Aside from causing mild eye and skin irritation, they have low mammalian toxici-ty. They are biodegradable. However, once they dry, they are no longer effective.

Attracting beneficial insects Creating an environment hostile to pests includes enlisting the help of benefi-cials. These insects keep undesirable pest popula-tions in check through their feeding, as either preda-tors or parasites. Both the adult and immature stages of predators actively search out and consume their prey. Parasites help you by depositing their eggs in or on the host prey. When these eggs hatch, the host becomes their food source.

What can you do to encourage helpful insects? Well, there's nothing like a nontoxic environment, a bit of nectar, a sip of water, and a protected spot to keep beneficials from wandering. Here's how to make your yard attractive to beneficials by looking after their basic needs:

First, avoid using pesticides. You don't want to harm the good guys, and you don't want to starve them by poisoning their favorite insect food sources. Second, beneficial insects are more likely to remain in your yard if you provide their favorite pollen and nectar sources. Common herbs such as fennel, dill, spearmint, caraway, coriander, and tansy would be a good start. While you're at it, plant a border that includes some wildflowers, such as yarrow and Queen Anne's lace, along with cos-mos and other flowering plants, that will provide a continuous succession of blooms.

Beneficials may like tasty herbs, such as coriander, as much as you do.

Water is also important and can be supplied by sinking a few shallow pans with small rocks in them into the soil. They will fill from rain or watering. Finally, places to shelter and overwinter can be provided by the addition of shrubs, vines, or small evergreens. If these sheltering plants include berry-bearing shrubs such as chokeberry, bayberry, sumacs, and viburnums, the fruits will attract grub-eating birds for additional pest control.

A Garden for Beneficials

Gardens designed to encourage high beneficial insect populations should incorporate a variety of flowering plants rich in nectar and pollen. Choose cultivars with easily accessible pollen, found in plants that have just a single layer of petals or a tubular flower form. Common herbs, wildflowers, and scented plants are all attractive to beneficial insects. Remember come fall that the dead foliage continues to be an important habitat for beneficials over the winter, so don't clear it out!

Downy yellow violet
(*Viola pubescens*)

Note: Blooming times will vary depending on cultivar, plant maturity, and location.

Spring

Columbine (*Aquilegia* species) Perennial blooming in early spring.
Rosemary (*Rosmarinus officinalis*) Perennial herb blooming in early spring.
Violet (*Viola* species) Perennial blooming in early spring.

Lemon balm
(*Melissa officinalis*)

Johnny jump up
(*Viola cornuta*)

Mossy stonecrop wallpepper
(*Sedum*)

Queen Anne's lace (*Daucus carota*) Biennial blooming from spring through summer.
Stonecrop (*Sedum* species) Perennial blooming spring through summer.
Blue salvia (*Salvia farinacea*) Annual blooming late spring through summer.
Dill (*Anethum graveolens*) Annual herb blooming late spring through summer.
Lemon balm (*Melissa officinalis*) Perennial herb blooming late spring through summer.
Tickseed (*Coreopsis* species) Perennial blooming from late spring through summer.
Thyme (*Thymus* species) Perennial herb blooming late spring through summer.

Golden thyme
(*Thymus* × *citriodorus*)

Summer

Coriander (*Coriandrum sativum*) Annual herb blooming in early summer.
Fennel (*Foeniculum vulgare*) Biennial herb blooming in summer.

Variegated sage 'Tricolor' (*Salvia officinalis*)

Cosmos (*Cosmos bipinnatus*)

Lavender (*Lavandula* species) Perennial herb blooming in summer.

Parsley (*Petroselinum crispum*) A biennial blooming in summer.

Sage (*Salvia officinalis*) Perennial herb blooming in summer.

Tansy (*Tanacetum vulgare*) Perennial herb blooming in summer.

Summer Into Fall

Marigold (*Tagetes* species) Annual blooming early summer into late fall.

Bee balm (*Monarda didyma*) Perennial blooming summer into fall.

Purple coneflower (*Echinacea purpurea*) Perennial blooming summer into fall.

Cosmos (*Cosmos bipinnatus*) Annual blooming summer into fall.

Cumin (*Cuminum cyminum*) Annual herb blooming summer into fall.

Goldenrod (*Solidago* species) Perennial blooming summer into fall.

Mint (*Mentha* species) Perennial herb blooming summer into fall.

Joe-Pye weed (*Eupatorium* species) Perennial blooming summer into fall.

Yarrow (*Achillea* species) Perennial blooming summer into fall.

Aster (*Aster* species) Perennial blooming late summer into late fall.

Chrysanthemum (*Chrysanthemum* species) Summer into late fall.

Nasturtium (*Tropaeolum* species) Annual blooming summer into late fall.

Nasturtiums (*Tropaeolum* species)

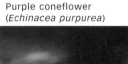
Purple coneflower
(*Echinacea purpurea*)

Marigolds (*Tagetes*)
Top 'Yellow boy'
Right 'Disco flame'
Bottom 'Little hero'

Bee balm
(*Monarda didyma*)

Horsemint (*Mentha longfolia*)

More Beneficials

Following are some insects that feed on lawn pests.

Lady beetle

Ground beetle

Lady beetles Ladybugs are perhaps the most widely recognized beneficial insects. As adults, and especially in the larval form, ladybugs feed on small soft-bodied insect pests, like aphids. Having short legs and antennae, adults are ¼ inch or smaller, oval, brightly colored, and often spotted. Their ravenous larvae resemble tiny alligators with flat gray bodies tapering to the tail, with red or orange spots.

Ground beetles Known as "caterpillar hunters," ground beetles are valuable nocturnal predators with a taste for beetle grubs, caterpillars, armyworms, and cutworms. These fast-moving creatures, ¾ to 1 inch long with flattened blue, black, or brown bodies spend their days hiding under stones and garden debris. Larvae are long, dark, and tapered, with segmented bodies.

Mantids These large green or brownish insects up to 4 inches long are called "praying mantids" or "mantis" after the position in which they hold their front legs. With big, bulging eyes and still posture, they are voracious predators who even eat their own young. While still considered beneficial, they are nonselective in choosing their prey and may consume helpful insects, including each other, as well as pests.

Lacewings Green to the east of the Rocky Mountains and brown to the west, these delicate ½- to ¾-inch-long insects, when at rest, hold their large, clear, and highly veined wings up like a tent.

Lacewings: **Top** adult **Bottom** larva

Their larvae are called "aphid lions," but they're not averse to eating other pests, like caterpillar eggs, leafhopper nymphs, or mites.

Big-eyed bugs Especially helpful where chinch bugs are a problem, this bulging-eyed ⅛- to ¼-inch-long black or gray insect also eats leafhoppers, mites, aphids, and caterpillars. Unlike most insect predators, the bugs in this family, Lygaeidae Geocoris species, have been known to take an occasional bite or two from plants. These beneficial insects are found across the United States.

Big-eyed bug

This sequence shows the hatching of a praying mantid egg case (far left), available for a few dollars by mail order. Over a two- to three-hour period, an egg case hatches 40-100 mantids less than ½ inch long (center left). Most quickly drop to cover; yet some, such as the upside-down mantid (near left), must first struggle to break free of the egg-case filaments still attached to their hind legs. Depending on the species, an adult praying mantid (below) may range in size from 1 to 4 inches.

Spined soldier bugs Unfortunately, this beneficial is often mistaken for its stink bug cousins, which are pests. This ½-inch-long lover of caterpillars, grubs, and fall army-worms has a shield-shaped body and is differentiated from stink bugs by pointed shoulders and a black mark on the wing membrane.

Braconid wasps These slender ⅒- to ½-inch parasitic wasps deposit eggs either inside of the host prey or in pupal cocoons on or near a dead host insect. In this way, a small species of braconid wasp parasitizes aphids, and a larger species parasitizes a wide variety of beetles, caterpillars, and other insects.

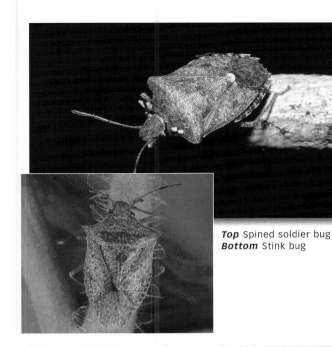

Top Spined soldier bug
Bottom Stink bug

Braconid wasp atop its pupal cocoons on caterpillar

PREDATORY NEMATODES

Beneficial predatory nematodes are microscopic members of the roundworm family that live in the soil but not usually in numbers high enough to offer much control of insect pests. Nematodes are now available from garden suppliers specializing in organic gardening products.

The most commonly used nematodes are from the Steinernematidae and Heterorhabditidae families. Killing their hosts within 48 hours, they offer control of surface pests, such as chinch bugs and sod webworms, as well as soil-dwelling pests, like billbugs and white grubs. Your choice of nematode should be based on the target pest's habitat. For moist-soil and deeper-dwelling pests (3 to 6 inches), heterorhabditid nematodes are the way to go. *Steinernema carpocapsae* is more effective on surface feeders because of its better mobility. *Steinernema glaseri* is used for soil dwellers. Research in Florida has shown another nematode, *Steinernema scapterisci*, to be effective in controlling mole cricket populations in that state.

Remember that nematodes are living organisms. They need moisture to keep them from drying out and to aid in their movement, so be sure to irrigate release areas before and after application. It is best to release nematodes at night, during warm weather, and when humidity is high and the soil temperature is 55° to 90°F.

Nematodes may arrive by mail in a sponge sealed in plastic (at right, on bucket). This sponge contains about 5 million dormant nematodes (*Heterorhabditis* species). Although 5 million may sound like enough for all the grubs in a golf course, that number handles only 300 square feet of lawn. Place the sponge in a container of cold water and wring it out several times to release the nematodes. Further dilute this solution and apply it with a watering can or a hose-end sprayer.

Moles in the Lawn

Insects aren't the only pests to bother lawns. Some four-footed varmints—moles—may also take up residence. You might first become aware that these small creatures are in your lawn when you nearly trip stepping into the soft earth of a tunnel. Moles create these passageways as they burrow underground in their almost constant search for food. Moles eat an estimated 40 pounds of insects a year and tunnel day and night looking for food. The dirt pushed up in this effort leaves a network of low ridges across the landscape and an occasional pile of surplus dirt—a molehill.

Moles are difficult to get rid of. A skilled mole-hunting dog or cat can keep a mole population down. But trapping is considered the most effective means of eliminating moles. Designed to kill moles in their tunnels, traps should be placed in main activity tunnels, not in the shallow, temporary branches. Main tunnels run underground at a depth of 1 to 5 inches. Because moles can't hibernate, winter tunnels can be more than 24 inches deep.

Where tunneling is visible, look for straight runs with branches coming off of them. Test for tunnels by caving in straight sections with your feet; then recheck several hours later to see if the tunnels have been rebuilt. Rebuilding indicates main thoroughfares. You can also find main tunnels by using a rod to probe the ground around mole-

Moles measure 4 to 6 inches in body length. They use their large forepaws to claw the soil aside and press it against tunnel side walls. Skilled people can capture moles alive, like this one, by shoveling up their quarry from the advancing end of a tunnel and depositing it in a bucket for transport to the wild. Spring-loaded traps aren't as merciful, but they can be effective; some traps impale moles from above and others crush the small creatures between pincers.

Moles build near-surface tunnels, as shown, and far deeper tunnels. Moles feed mainly on earthworms but also eat grubs and other small critters. They don't eat the roots and bulbs they displace during tunneling, but the roots and bulbs often dry out and die as a result. Mice and voles use the mole tunnels and feed on roots and bulbs, leaving moles to take the blame.

Above Although some people make mountains out of mole-hills, molehills may be a foot tall, giving them mountainlike stature in a lawn. They result when moles push soil up from their deeper underground tunnels. *Inset top* Each bare spot indicates the location of a former molehill that was tamped down. The pattern around the tree roots is characteristic.

Chipmunks burrow in lawns, but their doorways are barely noticeable, and their tunnels aerate the soil. Such critters are another reason to think twice before applying lawn toxins.

Synthetic Toxins: A Last Resort

In its consumer booklet *Citizen's Guide to Pest Control and Pesticide Safety*, the EPA states that healthy lawns will have some weeds and insect pests as well as beneficial insects and earthworms. The guide notes that following a preventive health-care program for your lawn should enable you to avoid most pesticide use.

It's important to think of turf diseases and insect damage as symptoms of a breakdown in your lawn's ecosystem rather than as problems to attack with toxins. When problems occur, your first step should be diagnosis, followed by an adjustment of your cultural practices to alleviate the causes. If treatment becomes necessary, start with mechanical and biological controls. Synthetic chemical products should be a last resort. Use of synthetics will provide only temporary relief, and unlike botanical toxins, many synthetics remain potent in the environment long after their application. They can contaminate ground water and kill off needed soil microorganisms and beneficial insects.

If you feel that your lawn pest problem is so serious that it warrants the use of synthetic chemicals, try to use the least toxic products you can and those that break down relatively quickly. Also, check with your Cooperative Extension Service for local recommendations.

hills. You will feel a sudden give when the rod pierces a tunnel. There are a number of traps on the market, and your choice will depend on the type of moles prevalent in your area. For trap sources, check with your local Cooperative Extension Service or garden-supply center.

Some people claim to have had success spraying affected areas with commercial mole repellents. Usually made from unrefined castor oil suspended in fatty acids, the products are said to emit an odor that moles don't like.

Another approach to the problem of moles is to lighten up and think about the positive things moles do for you. Their runways help aerate, loosen, and mix the soil, and their feeding keeps the larval populations of numerous turf pests in check. With this approach, though, you've got to remember to watch your step when you walk across the lawn!

SAFE PESTICIDE USE

- ❑ Use the least toxic, most target-specific, chemical.
- ❑ Purchase the smallest amount needed to do the job.
- ❑ Don't mix more spray than you need—and stick to target areas only.
- ❑ Read the label carefully, and follow all recommendations precisely.
- ❑ Wear protective clothing and gear as directed.
- ❑ Wear gloves when using a sprayer and wash well afterward.

- ❑ Do not use pesticides if rain is forecast or if it is windy.
- ❑ Launder pesticide-contaminated clothing separately.
- ❑ Keep leftover pesticides away from children.
- ❑ Keep leftover chemicals in their original containers.
- ❑ Call the National Pesticide Telecommunications Network (1-800-858-7378) for more information, or check out its web site at ace.orst.edu/info/nptn.

chapter 12

Ground Covers and Ornamental Grasses

European wild ginger

GROUND COVERS OFFER a low-maintenance alternative to lawns. Use them in low-traffic areas or in areas where grass doesn't thrive, such as in shady places or on slopes subject to erosion. Ground covers also form borders that help unify other plantings and accentuate walkways. In addition, ground covers can replace areas of lawn you are tired of maintaining.

The key to enjoying a long, untroubled relationship with these versatile plants is to make your selections carefully. The following list of popular ground covers should help you choose plants that will meet your landscape needs and, most importantly, thrive in your yard's environment.

Shade-Loving Ground Covers

Bishop's hat (*Epimedium × versicolor*) Able to hold its own with tree roots, bishop's hat has heart-shaped leaves held aloft on wiry stems. Clusters of tiny daffodil-like flowers (available in a variety of colors) appear in spring. Epimedium does best in acid soils with lots of humus but will tolerate dry shade. USDA Zones 5 to 8.

Bishop's hat

'Lavandelle' daylily

English ivy

English ivy (*Hedera helix*) Available in a host of cultivars and colors, from lustrous dark green to variegated, this well-known climber also makes a versatile ground cover. Preferring moist, rich soil in shade, ivy grows well under trees or down embankments where it is useful for erosion control, but it can be invasive. Algerian ivy (*H. canariensis*) is grown in California. USDA Zones 5 to 9.

European wild ginger (*Asarum europaeum*) Heart-shaped glossy dark green foliage makes this shade-loving evergreen a standout. With ample moisture and humus-rich soil, wild ginger forms a slow-spreading, dense mat. It is at home with hostas and ferns. USDA Zones 4 to 8.

Lily-of-the-valley (*Convallaria majalis*) Even in poor, dry soil, this old favorite can be found perfuming

Lily-of-the-valley

If you're looking to add grace, beauty, and color accents to your lawn—and reduce lawn maintenance—planting ornamental grasses and ground covers may be the answer.

Lilyturf

Hosta

Hosta with margined leaves

the air under trees and shrubs come spring. Lily-of-the-valley reproduces rapidly and should be planted in areas where it can be contained. USDA Zones 3 to 8.

Hosta, or plantain lily (*Hosta* species) Sporting ribbed leaves in a multitude of sizes and color variations, hostas have found a place in many a shaded yard. In midsummer, they put out spikes of tubular white or lavender flowers, fragrant in some species. Grow hostas as accent plants in average soil. USDA Zones 3 to 8.

Sweet woodruff (*Galium odoratum*) With its delicate whorls of light green foliage and clusters of starlike white flowers in spring, this plant thrives in moist, rich soil in light to dense shade. USDA Zones 3 to 8.

Ground Covers for Partial Shade to Sun

Bugleweed (*Ajuga reptans*) Growing best in shade, this potentially invasive plant will tolerate sunnier locations if given enough moisture. Ajuga requires little upkeep, forming dense low mats of either green, purplish, variegated, or bronze foliage, depending on the cultivar and time of year. Significant spikes of purple to violet flowers appear in spring. USDA Zones 3 to 8.

Bugleweed

Lilyturf (*Liriope* species) These popular grasslike perennials make excellent ground covers and attractive edgers. *Liriope muscari* (below) has dark green or variegated leaves and late-summer spikes of violet-blue flowers. *Liriope spicata* is hardier (to Zone 5) and tolerates salt spray, heat, and drought, but it is also more aggressive. USDA Zones 5 or 6 to 10.

Daylily (*Hemerocallis* species) It's hard to find fault with this large group of perennials. Daylilies grow taller than most ground covers but will spread to cover areas not subject to foot traffic.

Sweet woodruff

Lilyturf (*Liriope muscari*)

Wild daylily flowers

Daylily foliage

There are even low-growing evergreens for the South. Blooming best in bright sun, these easy-to-grow plants adapt to partial shade and varying soils. They come in a range of flower colors, heights, and blooming times. USDA Zones 3 to 9.

Pachysandra, or Japanese spurge (*Pachysandra terminalis*) Given well-drained, rich soil and a locale where the summers don't get too hot and dry, this widely grown evergreen perennial thrives even in dense shade and requires little upkeep. Its dark, glossy green leaves combine well with just about any other plant. A variegated form is also available. USDA Zones 4 to 8.

Mondo grass (*Ophiopogon planiscapus* 'Nigrescens') The arching purple-black foliage of this grasslike member of the lily family is outstanding. In areas with hot summers, plant mondo grass in a semi-shaded location where it will form low, thick mats if given rich, fertile soil and regular moisture. This cultivar is also called 'Ebony Knight' and 'Arabicus'; the species form is green. USDA Zones 5 to 10.

Periwinkle, or myrtle (*Vinca minor*) Frequently planted for decorative edgings under shrubs and around rocks, this hardy evergreen with trailing stems of oval glossy green leaves spends several months graced by small blue-violet flowers. Preferring shade and moderately moist soil, it will tolerate sunny conditions with adequate moisture. USDA Zones 3 to 9.

St. John'swort (*Hypericum species*) Evergreen in warm climates, this low-growing hardy shrub is covered with yellow blossoms in summer and has small dark green leaves. Not suited to extended hot weather, it thrives in sandy soil with moderate moisture. Some hypericums become invasive. USDA Zones 6 to 8.

Black mondo grass

'Variegata' Japanese pachysandra and Allegheny pachysandra

Periwinkle

St. John'swort

Sun-Loving Ground Covers

Dropmore scarlet honeysuckle

Cotoneaster (*Cotoneaster* species) Available in both evergreen and deciduous varieties, these woody shrubs have distinctive small bright red fruits, tiny oval leaves, and fanlike branches. Low-growing, spreading, and handsome cascading over rock walls (some will climb), they are also suited to well-drained banks and rock gardens. Leaves of deciduous varieties turn red in fall. USDA Zones 5 to 8.

Cotoneaster

Juniper (*Juniperus* species) Many gardeners feel that the low, spreading forms of this well-known evergreen, with its spreading branches of blue-green scalelike leaves, are the best ground covers for well-drained, hot, and sunny locations. There is a juniper for any situation where a drought-resistant, adaptable plant is needed. USDA Zones 3 to 9.

Honeysuckle (*Lonicera* × *brownii* 'Dropmore Scarlet') A woody vine that grows well in partial shade as well as in full sun, dropmore scarlet honeysuckle makes an attractive, sprawling ground cover. The vivid red flowers with yellow throats are long lasting. USDA Zones 4–9.

Stonecrop (*Sedum* species) Widely admired for their tough, succulent foliage and intriguing forms, there are myriad low-growing sedums from which to choose. Given full sun and well-drained soil, it's an excellent choice for rock gardens, walls, and crevices. USDA Zones 3 to 8.

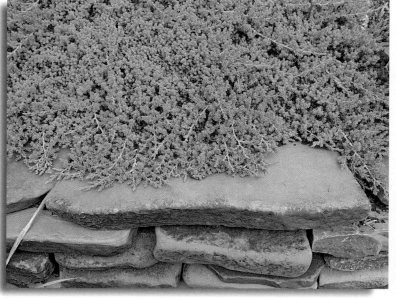

Juniper

Mossy stonecrop

Ornamental Grasses

Golden hakone grass (*Hakonechloa macra* 'Aureola') Placed in a shady location, this arching grass lights up a dark corner with its green-and-gold foliage. Forming slow-growing clumps, hakone grass grows best when kept moist in well-drained, fertile soil. USDA Zones 7 to 9.

Fountain grass

'Aureola' golden hakone grass

Japanese silver grass (*Miscanthus sinensis*) The many *Miscanthus* cultivars are arching, graceful grasses that develop decorative, feathery plumes in late summer to fall. Most of them prefer sunny spots that have rich, moist soil. Depending on the cultivar, they can grow quite tall. USDA Zones 5 to 9.

Fountain grass (*Pennisetum alopecuroides*) Given fertile, well-drained soil in a sunny to partially shady location, this densely tufted midsize grass with fine foliage is lovely to see in bloom. The striking, arching stalks bear soft, sand-colored to dark purple bottlebrush flowers in late summer. USDA Zones 5 to 9.

Northern sea oats (*Chasmanthium latifolium*) Preferring full sun up north and partial shade where summers get hot, this arching, loosely tufted, spreading grass has bamboolike foliage that turns a soft coppery tan in fall. The flat seed heads are excellent for flower arrangements. USDA Zones 5 to 9.

Blue fescue (*Festuca caesia* formerly *F. glauca*) Foot-high, spiky, silvery blue foliage makes this clump-forming grass a standout in sunny, well-drained locations. Adequate moisture and partial shade will keep it looking its best in warmer regions. USDA Zones 4 to 9.

Northern sea oats

'Yaku Jima' dwarf Japanese silver grass

'Elijah Blue' blue fescue

Lawn Tools

LAWN TOOLS FALL INTO three categories: tools you should own, tools helpful to own if you have the budget and space, and tools used so seldom they are best rented. The following recommendations assume average situations. Your needs may differ.

Tools to Own

The tools and machines in this group are essential to a good lawn-care program.

Mowers

Choose a lawn mower according to the size of your lawn, the terrain, your energy level, and your own feelings about noise and air quality.

Gasoline-powered rotary mower This lawn mower is currently the most popular. The single horizontal blade can cut through the toughest grass, and the four wheels allow you to mow a bumpy lawn without scalping it. Available in walk-behind, riding, or tractor designs, with options such as self-propulsion, grass catchers, and electric starters, these new mowers also produce less pollution than they did in former years, thanks to EPA standards. Gas engine emissions standards have required manufacturers to phase in cleaner-burning engines. These machines are reliable unless you commit the cardinal sin of leaving gas in the tank during the off-season. If you don't drain the gasoline prior to long-term storage, gumlike varnish deposits may form and cause starting problems or poor engine operation.

Gasoline-powered mulching mower Also called a recycling mower, this machine is similar to the rotary mower. Its specially shaped mower housing and blade work together to suspend clippings long enough for several passes with the blade, making the clippings fine enough to leave where they fall.

Reel mower Available in manual or gasoline-powered models, reel mowers have five or more horizontal blades that rotate in a cylindrical path, pressing grass against a cutting bar and making a scissorlike cut. Reel mowers give a cleaner cut than rotary mowers, and their blades stay sharp longer. But reel mowers are more susceptible to jamming from twigs and wet, heavy grass than rotary mowers are, and they are not well suited to tough-bladed grasses or to lawns with frequent dips and rises. Reel mowers generally have limited height adjustment, to a maximum of 1½ or 2 inches, making it impossible to cut grass at a greater height, and the blades must be sharpened by a professional. Also, the design of this machine does not allow the blades to reach to the outside width of the wheels, as the blades on most rotary mowers do, so reel mowers won't trim close along most lawn edges.

Electric mower These mowers come in corded or cordless models. Corded mowers are lightweight, but you need to drag a heavy power cord around as you mow. They are fine for small lawns with few obstacles. Cordless electrics free you from extension cords, thanks to improved battery technology. One charge in a cordless mower with a 36-volt battery will run for well over three hours doing light mowing or for about two hours doing heavier mowing. Compared with gas-powered models, electrics tend to have narrower cutting widths, which add to mowing time, but they make less noise, emit no noxious fumes, and require no engine maintenance, such as annual oil and spark-plug changes.

Gasoline-powered
mulching mower
(walk-behind)

Manual
reel mower

Gasoline-powered
tractor mower

Cordless
electric mower

Spreaders

Today's spreaders are usually made of lightweight plastic and are easy to operate. Precision of application is the main difference between the two types.

Drop spreader Drop spreaders distribute seed, fertilizer, and other amendments, such as lime, in swaths the width of the spreader. Settings allow you to control the amount distributed. This type of spreader is ideal for distributing its payload along edges, flower beds, and paths.

Rotary spreader A rotary spreader flings seed or amendments over a wide area, thereby covering ground faster than drop spreaders. However, it is not well suited for use on windy days or with small, irregularly shaped lawns.

Sprayers

You will need a sprayer for dispensing insecticidal soap or oil solutions. Sprayers are typically available in canister or backpack styles with 2- to 4-gallon polyethylene tanks and interchangeable nozzles for varying application patterns and rates.

Hand Tools

Spade Often mistakenly called shovels, spades have flat or gently curved blades and are used for planting or transplanting, for edging, and for removal of weeds and old turf.

Round-point shovel These are designed to move large quantities of fine-textured material, such as sand, soil, or nonfibrous mulches, from one place to another. But they can serve quite well digging soil too.

Garden rake The steel-headed type is useful for preparing small areas of soil for the planting of seed, plugs, or sprigs.

Lawn-and-leaf rake Those rakes with an extra-wide head make the work go faster but require more muscle. Bamboo rakes are usually the lightest and easiest to use. Typically, however, they last only a few seasons before falling apart. Steel rakes and the modern plastics can be durable.

Landscape rake This has a wide, 36-inch aluminum head mounted on an aluminum or wood shaft. Use it to remove debris from prepared soil and to level the soil prior to planting a new lawn.

SPREADERS AND SPRAYERS

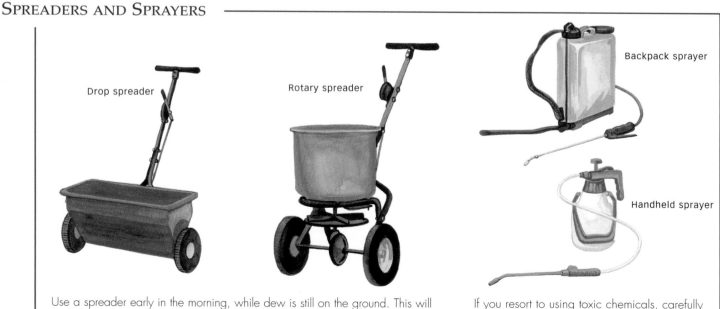

Drop spreader

Rotary spreader

Backpack sprayer

Handheld sprayer

Use a spreader early in the morning, while dew is still on the ground. This will help you avoid skips because wheel tracks are easier to see on the wet grass.

If you resort to using toxic chemicals, carefully follow manufacturer precautions.

Thatching rake The thatching, or dethatching, rake is made primarily for removing thatch from your lawn without damaging the structure of the turf. The angle of the rake head can be adjusted by means of nuts to control the depth of tine penetration and to suit your height.

Pruning tools Keep several types on hand for various situations. Use one-hand pruning shears for twigs and branches up to ½ inch; lopping shears for ½- to 1½-inch branches; pruning saws for woody branches up to 3 inches in diameter; and a bow saw or chain saw for larger branches.

HAND TOOLS

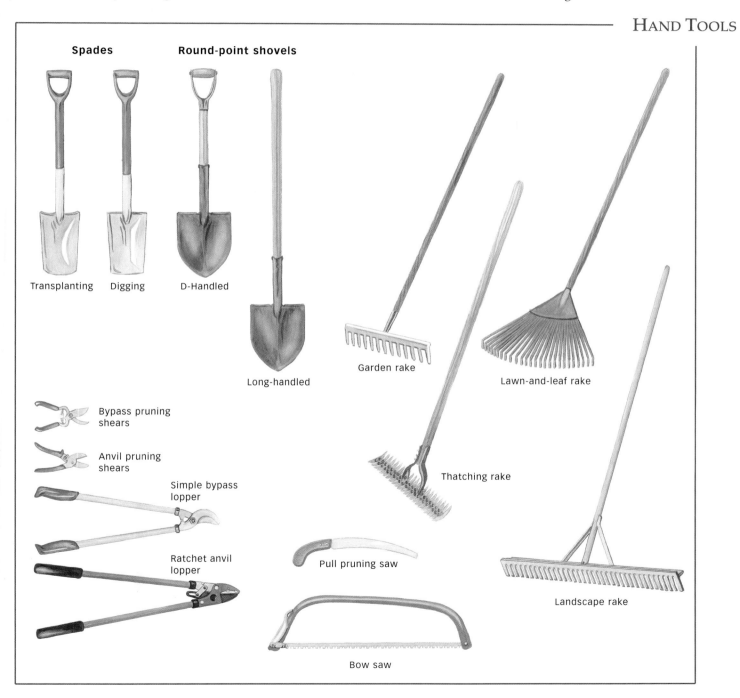

Spades
Transplanting   Digging

Round-point shovels
D-Handled

Long-handled

Garden rake

Lawn-and-leaf rake

Thatching rake

Landscape rake

Bypass pruning shears

Anvil pruning shears

Simple bypass lopper

Ratchet anvil lopper

Pull pruning saw

Bow saw

Manual aerator Foot-powered and easy to use, a manual aerator is fine if you have a small lawn and time on your hands. But you'll regret attempting to aerate a large lawn with this slow-going tool. (See a power aerator on page 149.)

Grape (grubbing) hoe This wide, heavy-bladed hoe offers a low-tech but surprisingly efficient way to remove turf you no longer want.

Grass shears Shears provide a time-honored but slow means of clipping grass along the edge of a garden bed. Clipping with shears is valuable where your prized flowers grow too close to the path of an indiscriminate string trimmer.

Weeder The forked steel head on a short hardwood handle allows the prying of weeds from turf.

Turf edger A half-moon-shaped steel cutting head is mounted to a hardwood handle. Use it to keep lawn edges neat or to trim away excess when laying sod along irregular lawn edges.

Garden carts and wheelbarrows These indispensable aids haul everything from lawn tools and fertilizer to weeds and prunings.

MORE HAND TOOLS

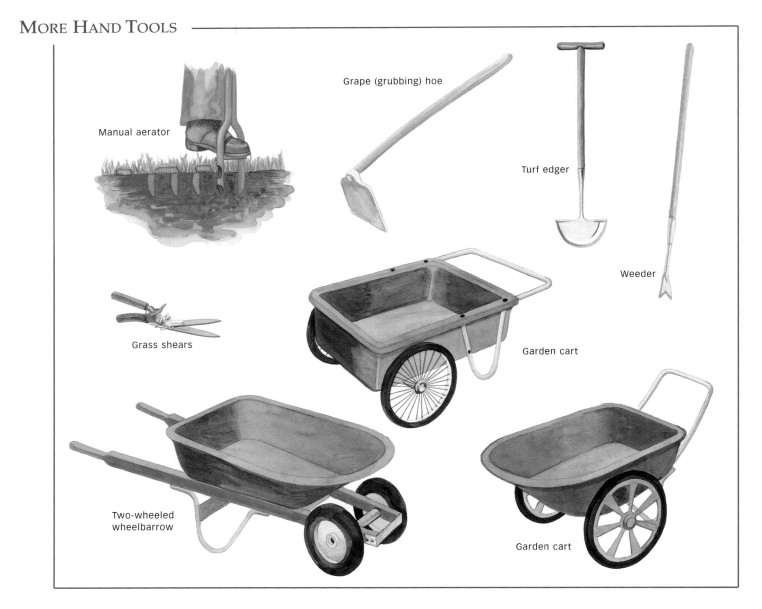

Manual aerator

Grape (grubbing) hoe

Turf edger

Weeder

Grass shears

Garden cart

Two-wheeled wheelbarrow

Garden cart

Specialty Tools

The following tools are convenient to own if your budget and storage space allow.

Power edger This is a gasoline-powered tool with a short blade that you can use horizontally to trim grass at lawn edges or vertically to create and maintain edges.

String trimmer There are gas-, electric-, and battery-powered models. Plastic line at the cutting end rotates at high speed to trim grass or weeds along lawn edges and near fixtures such as lampposts and fences. The better-balanced and easier-to-use models have the power unit at the top end of a long shaft and an adjustable handle in the middle. As the line wears or breaks, you feed more line by tapping the cutting head on the ground. Excess line is sheared off by a small blade built into the debris guard. Cutting swaths range from 6 to 10 inches for cordless units, 8 to 10 inches for corded electric models, and 15 to 18 inches for larger, heavier, gas-powered units.

Pole trimmer This is a pruning saw at the end of a 12-foot telescoping pole. It's great for homeowners who like to do high pruning with their feet firmly planted on the earth; it's also available with lopping shears.

Blower Powered by gas or electricity, this machine blows leaves into piles for easier collection. Blowers are available in either hand-held, wheeled, or backpack styles, the last two types leaving you less tired on big jobs. Even if you like raking leaves on the lawn, you'll appreciate a blower's help in moving leaves out from under shrubs. Drawbacks include noise, noxious emissions of gas-powered units, and difficulty of use on windy days.

Chain saw For the cutting of tree limbs and trunks larger than a few inches in diameter in an average-size yard, an electric saw can be a smarter buy than a gas-powered saw. If you can keep all your cutting within 100 feet or so of an outdoor electrical outlet protected by a ground-fault circuit interrupter, this is all the saw you'll need, even for cutting firewood.

SPECIALTY TOOLS

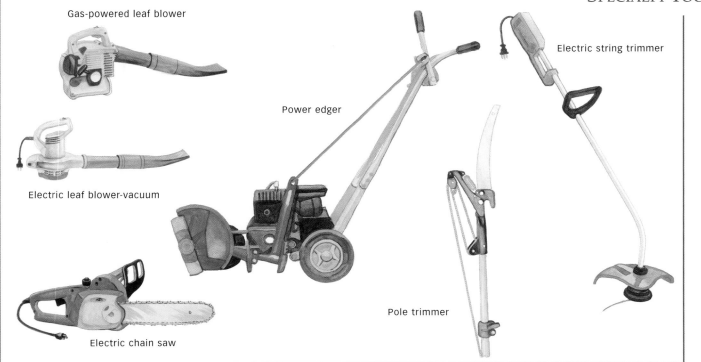

Gas-powered leaf blower

Electric leaf blower-vacuum

Power edger

Electric string trimmer

Pole trimmer

Electric chain saw

In contrast to bigger, heavier, gas-powered chain saws, electric saws emit no exhaust fumes and are low maintenance, low cost, and quiet operating. They are always ready to go, except that the chain needs sharpening whenever it begins to show signs of dulling, just like that of a gas-powered saw. Simple sharpening jigs are available for about the price of a saw chain. The jigs mount on the saw bar and allow you to sharpen each cutter at the same precise angle. This results in smooth wood cutting. (A dull chain produces sawdust-size particles and tempts you to mistakenly apply more bar pressure to the wood. A sharp chain yields wood chips that resemble dry oatmeal and cuts through wood almost as though it were butter.)

Caution: Of all the do-it-yourself tools described here, the chain saw is probably the most dangerous in the hands of inexperienced, fatigued, or careless people. The prime hazard is deep, bone-cutting injury resulting from saw kickback, which can occur when the chain arcing around the nose of the bar unexpectedly hits resistance, such as an unnoticed limb or other obstruction. To avoid kickback, always hold the saw by both handles with a firm grip and with your left elbow extended, not bent. With such a grip you will easily be able to control a kickback force, which feels more like a modest upward surge of the saw bar when you are in proper control. Also, keep the plane of the cutting chain aside from your body parts; then in the event of a surprise kickback, you will be out of the way.

Tools to Rent

Some of the tools in this group are expensive; others take up a lot of space and aren't needed often. So you are better off renting instead of buying these tools.

Power aerator Available in several styles, aerators loosen compacted soil by making many small holes in it. The best units have hollow coring devices that lift plugs of soil and turf from the lawn as the unit passes over it. These soil plugs quickly break apart and disappear, returning nutrients to the surface. Other somewhat less-effective units create holes by pushing spikes into the lawn.

Power tiller These are available in many styles and capacities, from small soil mixers to large 8-horse-power units. The tines churn soil and propel the machine forward. Larger units have the tines in the back and can dig deeper. When you pull back on the handles, the tiller digs deeper; when you lighten up on the handles, the tiller moves forward. Tillers are ideal for alleviating compaction in preparation for a new lawn or for mixing in soil amendments, such as lime, fertilizer, and compost. Some tillers are available with power rake and aerating attachments.

Lawn roller This is a metal drum with handles. Fill the drum about one-third full with water, and roll it on prepared soil to firm the soil and squeeze out excess air. Although this is a simple, inexpensive tool, it does take up storage space. Thus, you may want to rent it the few times you may need it.

Power dethatcher (lawn comber) This gas-powered tool has heavy, metal tines that whip the lawn as you pass the machine over it. Power rakes are great for removing light thatch and for prepping a lawn for overseeding.

Vertical mower Resembling a lawn mower, a vertical mower is useful for dethatching and for scarifying the soil in preparation for seeding. (See page 67.) This mower has several vertically mounted blades that are set to slightly penetrate the soil. If your lawn has heavy thatch, the blades may need to be set higher.

Power seeder (slit seeder) Similar to the vertical mower, this gasoline-powered unit (not shown) cuts many shallow grooves in prepared soil or turf and sows grass seed into them at recommended rates.

Sod cutter Four-wheeled and gasoline-powered, this machine has a horizontal reciprocating blade that cuts turf at the roots. You can then roll up the turf and save it for later use or simply compost it.

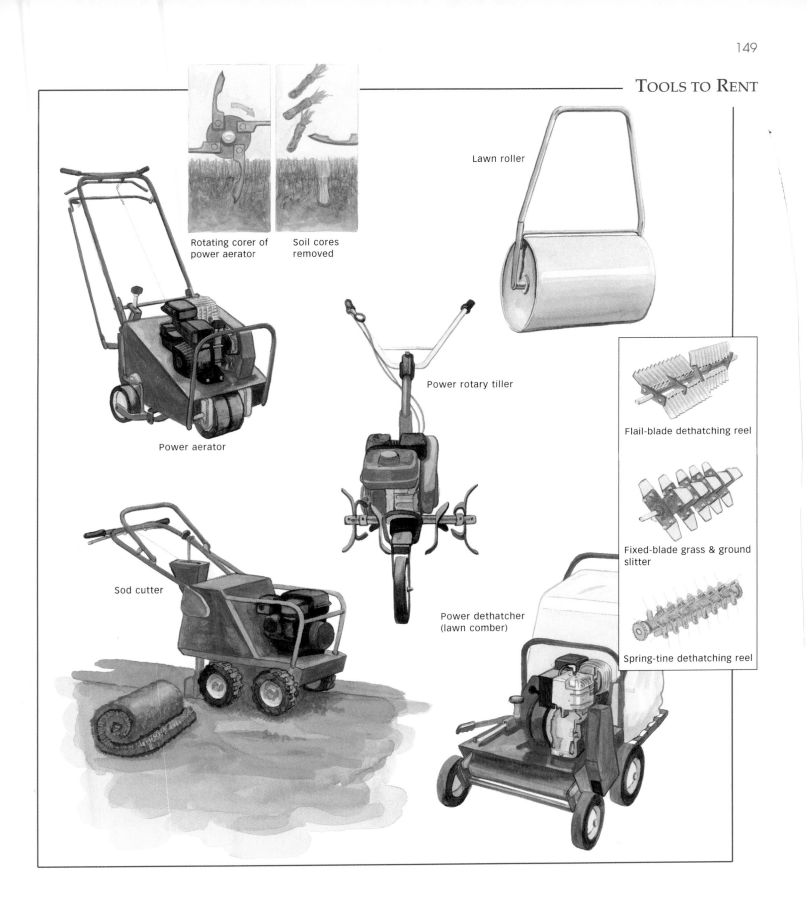

Rotating corer of power aerator

Soil cores removed

Lawn roller

Power aerator

Power rotary tiller

Flail-blade dethatching reel

Fixed-blade grass & ground slitter

Sod cutter

Power dethatcher (lawn comber)

Spring-tine dethatching reel

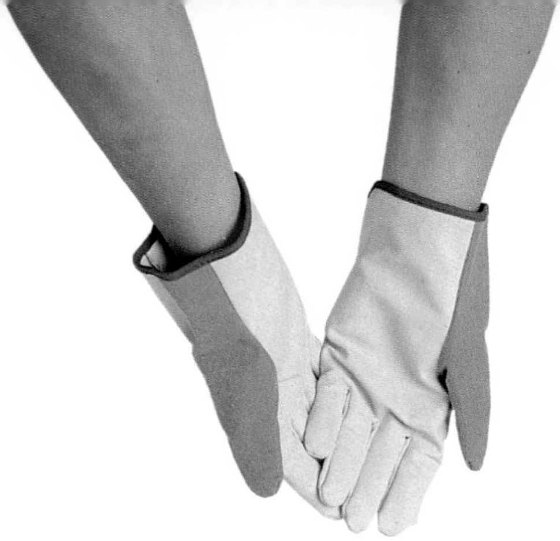

Sources for Lawn Management Information

The organizations listed below have agreed to be included here as sources of information.

Bio-Integral Resource Center (BIRC)
P.O. Box 7414
Berkeley, CA 94707

A nonprofit institution providing education and research on integrated pest management (IPM). Produces pest management publications and videos on IPM and lawns. Ask for a free catalog of publications and services.

Cooperative Extension Service (see next entry)

Cooperative State Research, Education, and Extension Service (CSREES)
U.S. Department of Agriculture
CSREES, Rm. 3328-South Building
Washington, D.C. 20250-0907

http://www.reeusda.gov/new/statepartners/usa.htm

The Cooperative Extension Service is part of CSREES, which augments its original mission: to offer educational outreach to people in a variety of areas, among them agricultural and natural resources. Through its extension agents, numerous publications, and Master Gardener phone information lines, Cooperative Extension Services offer many resources on lawn care.

To contact your local Cooperative Extension Service, try dialing information. In telephone directories, try subheadings under "County Government," such as "Agriculture," "Food," "Parks," or "Resource Management." The words *Cooperative Extension* may not be part of the listing. Also, farm groups, 4-H Clubs, or your state Agricultural Department may provide leads.

A national directory of Cooperative Extension services, *County Agents Directory*, is available in many public libraries. You can also find a state and county directory on the Internet at the Web site address above.

Gardens Alive!
5100 Schenley Place
Lawrenceburg, IN 47025

Supplier of organic lawn-care products, including grass seed mixtures, fertilizers, and weed- and pest-control products. Also sells beneficial insects and microorganisms featured in this book. Write for a free catalog.

Guelph Turfgrass Institute
328 Victoria Road South
Guelph, Ontario, Canada
N1H 6H8

http://www.uogueplh.ca/GTI
e-mail: info@gti.uoguelph.ca

Primarily serves professional turf managers. But for information pertinent to homeowners, visit its Web page. Also publishes a free brochure for homeowners on lawn care.

The Lawn Institute
http://www.lawninstitute.com

A nonprofit corporation that disseminates information on lawn care. Publishes *Lawn and Landscape Digest,* an excellent on-line quarterly.

National Coalition Against the Misuse of Pesticides (NCAMP)
701 E Street, S.E., Suite 200
Washington, DC 20003

A nonprofit group that provides information on pesticides and promotes reduced pesticide exposure.

National Turfgrass Evaluation Program
BARC – West
Building 2, Room 013
Beltsville, MD 20705

http://www.ntep.org/ntep
e-mail: kmorris@asrr.arsusda.gov

Tests, evaluates, and identifies turf grass species with improved qualities. Individuals can join the NTEP for a small fee and receive its annual Progress Report.

Natural Insect Control (NIC)
R.R. #2, Stevensville, Ontario, Canada
L0S 1S0

http://www.natural-insect-control.com
e-mail: nic@niagara.com

Mail-order supplier. Catalog includes organic fertilizers and environmentally friendly pest-control products.

Northwest Coalition for Alternatives to Pesticides
P.O. Box 1393
Eugene, OR 97440

http://www.efn.org/~ncap
e-mail: info@pesticide.org

An advocacy group that provides information on pesticides and offers alternatives to their use. It also publishes the *Journal of Pesticide Reform.*

Peaceful Valley Farm Supply
P.O. Box 2209
Grass Valley, CA 95945

http://www.groworganic.com

Mail-order supplier. Catalog features tools and supplies for organic farming and gardening—including in-ground irrigation supplies.

Rachel Carson Council, Inc.
8940 Jones Mill Road
Chevy Chase, MD 20815

http://members.aol.com/rccouncil/ourpage/rcc_page.htm
e-mail: rccouncil@aol.com

Dedicated to carrying on the work of Rachel Carson, this group maintains a library and clearinghouse of materials dealing with pesticide use and alternative forms of pest control and produces related publications.

Verdant Brands (formerly Ringer Corp.)
9555 James Ave. South, Suite 200
Bloomington, MN 55431-2543

http://www.verdantbrands.com

Manufacturer of Safer brand natural lawn-care products. Will answer questions about its products.

Glossary

Severe-weather brick
edging on sand
and gravel

Acid soil Soil with a pH measure below 7, also called sour soil. Most soils in the eastern third of the United States and Canada and along the West Coast are naturally acid.

Aeration (also called core cultivation or aerifying) Introduction of air to compacted soil by mechanically removing plugs of topsoil. Aeration helps oxygen, water, fertilizer, and organic matter to reach roots.

Alkaline soil Soil with a pH measure above 7, also called sweet soil. Many central and western states have alkaline soils.

Amendments Organic or mineral materials, such as peat moss, compost, or perlite, that are used to improve the soil.

Annual A plant that germinates, grows, flowers, produces seeds, and dies in the course of a single growing season. Annual grasses are sometimes used as nurse crops, to protect slower-growing seed, or to overseed warm-season grasses, during their dormancy.

Cool-season grasses Grasses that thrive in northern areas, including Canada, and in high elevations in the South.

Compost Humus made by decomposing vegetative matter in a compost bin or pile.

Crown The part of a plant where the roots and stem meet, usually at soil level.

Cultivar A *culti*vated *vari*ety of a plant, often bred for a desirable trait, such as pest- or disease-resistance.

Drainage The movement of water through the soil. With good drainage, water disappears from a planting hole in less than a few hours. If water remains standing overnight, drainage is poor.

Edging A shallow trench or physical barrier of metal, wood, brick, or synthetic material used to define the border between lawn turf and another area, such as paving or a flower bed.

Endophytes Fungi that live in some grasses (called endophytic) and make them harmful or deadly to a variety of aboveground grass-eating insects.

Exposure The intensity, duration, and variation in sun, wind, and temperature that characterize any particular lawn or planting site.

Frost heave, frost heaving A disturbance or uplift of soil, pavement, or plants caused by moisture in the soil freezing and expanding.

Full shade A site that receives no direct sun during the growing season.

Full sun A site that receives at least eight hours of direct sun each day during the growing season.

Grade The degree and direction of slope on an area of ground.

Ground cover A plant, such as ivy, liriope, or juniper, used to cover the soil and form a continuous low mass of foliage. Often used as a substitute for turf grass.

Hardiness A plant's ability to survive the winter without protection from the cold.

Hardiness zone A region where the coldest temperature in an average winter falls within a certain range, such as between 0° and –10°F.

Heat zone A region determined by the average annual number of days its temperatures climb above 86°F.

Herbicide A chemical used to kill plants. Preemergent herbicides are used to kill weed seeds as they sprout and thus to prevent weed growth. Postemergent herbicides kill plants that are already growing.

Humus Thoroughly decayed organic matter. Added to lawns, it will increase a soil's water-holding capacity, improve aeration, and support beneficial microbial life in the soil.

Invasive A plant that spreads quickly, usually by runners, and mixes with or dominates adjacent plantings.

Landscape fabric A synthetic fabric that is usually water-permeable, it is spread under paths or mulch to serve as a weed barrier.

Landscape fabric

Lawn restoration Improving a lawn without killing or removing all the existing turf.

Lime, limestone A white or grayish mineral compound used to combat soil acidity and to supply calcium for plant growth.

Loam An ideal soil type for growing, loam contains an equal balance of sand, silt, and clay.

Mass planting Filling an area with one or a few kinds of plants, such as ground covers, spaced closely together. Often planted to create a bold, dramatic effect or to reduce lawn maintenance.

Microclimate Conditions of sun, shade, exposure, wind, drainage, and other factors that affect plant growth at any particular site.

Mowing strip A row of bricks or paving stones set flush with the soil around the edge of a lawn area and wide enough to support the wheels on one side of a lawn mower.

Mulch A layer of bark, peat moss, compost, shredded leaves, hay or straw, lawn clippings, gravel, paper, plastic, or other material spread over the soil around the base of plants. During the growing season, mulch can help retard evaporation, inhibit weeds, and moderate soil temperature. In the winter, a mulch of evergreen boughs, coarse hay, or leaves is used to protect plants from freezing.

Native A plant that occurs naturally in a particular region and was not introduced from some other area.

Node A joint in grass plants from which leaves emerge.

Nurse grasses Annual grasses used to protect perennial grasses from excess wind and sun while they are becoming established.

Nutrients Nitrogen, phosphorus, potassium, calcium, magnesium, sulfur, iron, and other elements needed by growing plants and supplied by minerals and organic matter in soil and by fertilizers.

Organic matter Plant and animal residues, such as leaves, trimmings, and manure, in various stages of decomposition.

Overseeding Spreading seed over established turf that has been prepared for restoration.

Perennial grasses Grasses that persist year after year, given the right conditions.

Plugs Small round or square pieces of sod that can be planted to establish new lawns.

Pressure-treated lumber Lumber treated with chemicals that protect it from decay.

Retaining wall A wall built to stabilize a slope and keep soil from sliding or eroding downhill.

Rhizomes Underground runners of some types of plants that extend laterally to create new plants.

Selective pruning Using pruning shears to remove or cut back the branches of woody plants, usually to give the lawn greater sun exposure.

Sod Carpetlike sheets of turf about ¾ inch thick, 1½ feet wide, and 6 feet long. Strips may be laid over prepared soil to establish new lawns.

Sprigs Cut-up lengths of rhizomes or stolons (above- and underground runners) that can be broadcast and pressed into the soil to establish new lawns.

Stolons Aboveground runners from which some grasses, particularly warm-season varieties, spread.

Subsoil A light-colored soil layer usually found beneath the topsoil. It contains little or no humus.

Thatch A matlike buildup of grass roots and stems (but not of grass blade clippings) that if too thick can inhibit healthy growth.

Tiller

Stolon

Rhizome

Imaginary grass plant

Tillers Aboveground sideshoots of some types of grass plants. Bunch grasses spread (enlarge) through growth of tillers.

Warm-season grasses Grasses that grow best in southern regions, thriving in the heat of summer.

Weed Any undesirable plant or grass species.

Index

Note: Page numbers in **bold italic** refer to pages on which the subject is illustrated.

Metric Equivalents

All measurements in this book are given in U.S. Customary units. If you wish to find metric equivalents, use the following tables and conversion factors.

Inches to Millimeters and Centimeters

1 inch = 25.4 mm. = 2.54 centimeters

in	mm	cm
1/16	1.5875	0.1588
1/8	3.1750	0.3175
1/4	6.3500	0.6350
3/8	9.5250	0.9525
1/2	12.7000	1.2700
5/8	15.8750	1.5875
3/4	19.0500	1.9050
7/8	22.2250	2.2225
1	25.4000	2.5400

Inches to Centimeters and Meters

1 inch = 2.54 centimeters = 0.0254 meter

in	cm	m
1	2.54	0.0254
2	5.08	0.0508
3	7.62	0.0762
4	10.16	0.1016
5	12.70	0.1270
6	15.24	0.1524
7	17.78	0.1778
8	20.32	0.2032
9	22.86	0.2286
10	25.40	0.2540
11	27.94	0.2794
12	30.48	0.3048

Feet to Meters

1 foot = 0.3048 meter

ft	m
1	0.3048
5	1.5240
10	3.0480
25	7.6200
50	15.2400
100	30.4800

Square Feet to Square Meters

1 square foot = 0.092 903 04 square meter

Acres to Square Meters

1 acre = 4046.85642 square meters

Cubic Yards to Cubic Meters

1 cubic yard = 0.764 555 cubic meter

Ounces and Pounds (Avoirdupois) to Grams

1 ounce = 28.349 523 grams
1 pound = 453.5924 grams

Pounds to Kilograms

1 pound = 0.453 592 37 kilogram

Ounces and Quarts to Liters

1 ounce = 0.029 573 53 liter
1 quart = 0.9463 liter

Gallons to Liters

1 gallon = 3.785 411 784 liters

Fahrenheit to Celsius (Centigrade)

Celsius = Fahrenheit − 32 × 5/9

°F	°C
-30	-34.45
-20	-28.89
-10	-23.34
-5	-20.56
0	-17.78
10	-12.22
20	-6.67
30	-1.11
32 (freezing)	0.00
40	4.44
50	10.00
60	15.56
70	21.11
80	26.67
90	32.22
100	37.78
212 (boiling)	100

Photo Credits

Author Acknowledgments
The authors wish to thank the following for providing tools and equipment shown in photographs in this book:

The Toro Company, Minneapolis, MN; Isser & Associates, Public Relations, representing Ames Lawn & Garden Tools, Parkersburg, WV and A.H. Hoffman, Inc., manufacturer of potting soils, Lancaster, PA

Special Publisher Acknowledgments
Creative Homeowner Press wishes to thank the following facilities for allowing CHP staff to photograph their plants and grounds for publication. Credits follow alphabetically by facility:

Agnes Staab Garden & Greenhouse, Wingdale, NY: 33 (all three), 132 (bottom leftmost three)

Bloomingfields Farm (Daylilies), Gaylordsville, CT: 137 ('Lavendelle' daylily)

Claire's Garden Center, Patterson, NY: 131 (bee balm), 138 (hosta inset)

Ernest Hemingway Home, Key West, FL: 61 (top left),

Hollandia Nursery and Garden Center, Bethel, CT: 140 (honeysuckle)

Meadowbrook Farms, New Milford, CT: 130 (Johnny jump ups)

Photo Sources
Agricultural Research Service, USDA: 54

American Horticultural Society, Alexandria, VA: 55

American Phytopathological Society, St. Paul, MN: 117 (bottom left, bottom left inset, bottom right, bottom right inset), 118 (right, right inset)

Dr. Shirley Anderson, University of Florida, Gainesville: 61 (top right, bottom left), 62 (right), 63 (right)

Animals, Animals/Earth Scenes/Ken Cole, Chatham/New York, NY: 133 (top left)

Bluebird International, Inc., Englewood, CO: 67 (inset), 79 (bottom right)

Rita Buchanan, Winsted, CT: 110 (center left), 111 (right)

Crandall & Crandall, Dana Point, CA: 14 (middle inset, top inset), 23 (bottom), 38 (right), 39 (right, inset top, inset bottom), 72 (bottom left), 138 (bottom right), back cover (center right)

Dembinsky Photo Association, Owosso, MI, Joe Sroka: 8 (inset); Richard Shiell: 140 (top left), 141 (bottom right)

Alan & Linda Detrick, Glen Rock, NJ: 119 (bottom), 137 (top right)

Catriona Tudor Erler, Vienna, VA: 27 (top), 114 (right)

Gardens Alive!, Lawrenceburg, IN: 128, 133 (right center)

Grant Heilman, Lititz, PA: 123 (bottom center), 125 (bottom right inset)

John Colwell: 120–121 (large photo)

Jane Grushow: 23 (top right), 136–137 (large photo), 139 (bottom left), 141 (top left, bottom left)

Dr. Ray Kriner: 122 (bottom right, bottom right inset)

Larry Lefever: 2–3, 13 (top), 14–15 (large photo), 50–51 (large photo), 86 (top), 136 (left)

Lefever/Grushow: 8–9, 26 (left) 136 (inset), 138 (top), 141 (top right)

Barry L. Runk: 28–29 (soil types), 90-91 (large photo) 123 (top right), 125 (top left), 137 (bottom right)

Runk/Schoenberger: 6 (top right), 10 (inset), 104–105 (dandelions), 109 (bottom right, inset), 117 (top), 120

(inset), 121 (top), 122 (top), 124 (all), 125 (bottom left), 127 (left), 129 (top), 130 (bottom right), 132 (top left, middle right), 133 (bottom right)

Arthur C. Smith: 132 (top right)

Stanley/Schoenberger: 113 (inset), 116

Jim Strawser: 109 (bottom left), 111 (left), 125 (bottom right inset), 139 (center right)

Parwinder Grewal, Ohio State, Wooster: 127 (top right)

Dwight Kuhn, Dexter, MA: 6 (center left), 7 (top left, center right) 75 (all), 110 (dandelion flower and taproot), 123 (bottom left, bottom right, bottom right inset), 125 (top left inset), 132 (bottom right), back cover (top left)

Dr. Peter Landschoot, Penn State, University Park: 6 (top left, bottom left), 52, 59 (all), 60 (all), 62, 109 (top left), 112 (inset), 112-113 (large photo), 114 (left), 115, 118 (top left, bottom left), 119 (top left, center right)

Janet Loughrey Photography, Portland, OR: 16, 27 (bottom), 138 (bottom left), 139 (top right, bottom right) 141 (center right)

Mount Vernon Ladies' Association, Mount Vernon, VA: 10–11 (large photo)

Stephen E. Munz, Oradell, NJ: 5 (all), 150

L.R. Nelson, Peoria, IL: 94 (all), 96, 98, 99 (top)

North Wind Picture Archives, Alfred, ME: 11 (right) , 12 (top)

Jerry Pavia, Bonners Ferry, ID: 9 (top)

Robert Perron, Branford, CT: 13 (bottom), 26 (right)

Joe Provey, Fairfield, CT: 23 (top left), 28 (inset), 49 (top), 53 (all), 92

Renald Provey/Joe Provey, Fairfield, CT: 46, 47 (all), 79 (top, bottom left) 81 (top left)

Philip Rosenlund, Cheyenne, WY: 65 (left)

Susan A. Roth, Stony Brook, NY: 129 (bottom)

James P. Rowan, Chicago, IL: 132 (left center)

Tom Schmidt, "The Moleman," Cincinnati, OH: 134 (all)

Paul Schumm/CHP: 15 (top)

Neil Soderstrom, Wingdale, NY: 12 (bottom), 18 (top), 31 (bottom), 33 (all), 40, 41, 42, 42–43 (large photo), 45 (right), 57, 61 (top left), 99 (bottom), 101, 104 (insets left), 105 (inset), 107 (mid right), 110 (top left, bottom left, bottom right, top right), 127 (bottom), lower left, lower left insets, top right, top right inset), 130–131 (all), 132, bottom leftmost three), 133 (bottom), 135, 137 (top left inset, top right inset), 138 (top left inset, top right), 139 (daylilies, periwinkle inset)140 (top right, two bottom right)

Carl Weese, Fairfield, CT: author photo

Carl Weese/Joe Provey, Fairfield, CT: 7 (top right, bottom), 22 (all), 24, 30 (all), 31 (top, center left, center right), 34,35 (all), 38 (left, center), 39 (left), 43 (top, inset), 44 (all), 49 (bottom), 66–67 (large photo), 68 (all), 69 (all), 71 (all), 72 (top left, inset right, bottom inset), 73 (all), 74, 76–77 (large photo), 77 (middle inset), 78, 80 (all), 81 (bottom), 82 (all), 83 (all), 84–85 (all), 87 (all), 89 (all), 90 (inset), 91 (inset), 92 (all), 95 (all), 101, 103, 106 (both), 107 (top, bottom inset), 108, 109 (top), 140 (bottom left), back cover (top right)

Steve Wiest/Jack Fry, Kansas State, Manhattan: 64, 65 (right)

Karen Williams, University of Florida, Ft. Lauderdale: 61 (bottom right), 63 (left), 77 (top inset), 86 (bottom), 88 (all)

Have a home gardening, decorating, or improvement project? Look for these and other fine Creative Homeowner books at your local home center or bookstore. . .

Complete houseplant guide. 200 readily available plants; more than 400 photos. 192 pp.; 9"×10"
BOOK #: 275243

How to select and care for landscaping plants. Over 500 illustrations. 208 pp.; 9"×10"
BOOK #: 274238

Grow both decorative and edible plants. 400 photos/drawings. 176 pp.; 9"×10"
BOOK #: 274244

Four Regions: Northeast (274618); Mid-Atlantic (274537); Southeast (274762); Midwest (274385). 400 illustrations each.

Learn how to make the most of color. More than 150 color photos. 176 pp.; 9"×10"
BOOK #: 287264

How to create kitchen style like a pro. Over 150 color photographs. 176 pp.; 9"×10"
BOOK #: 279935

How to work with space, color, pattern, texture. Over 300 photos. 256 pp.; 9"×10"
BOOK #: 279667

All you need to know about designing a bath. Over 150 color photos. 176 pp.; 9"×10"
BOOK #: 287225

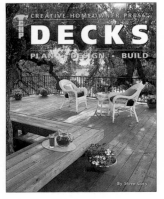

Step-by-step deck building for the novice. Over 500 color illustrations. 176 pp.; 8^1/$_2$"×10^7/$_8$"
BOOK #: 277180

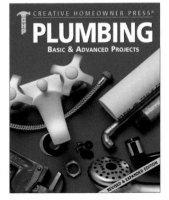

Best-selling house-wiring manual. More than 350 color illustrations. 160 pp.; 8^1/$_2$"×11"
BOOK #: 277048

Take the guesswork out of plumbing repair. More than 550 illustrations. 176 pp.; 8^1/$_2$"×10^7/$_8$"
BOOK#: 277620

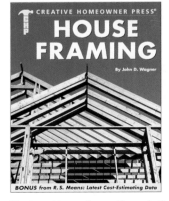

Designed to walk you through the framing basics. Over 400 illustrations. 240 pp.; 8^1/$_2$"×10^7/$_8$"
BOOK#: 277655